FLEISCHER SCHOL ~~ARS PROGRAM~~

Changing Lives Through Business Education

BUILDING
YOUR
MENTAL BALANCE
SHEET

BY

Morton H. Fleischer

Dedication

This book is dedicated first to my Mother and Father, who provided me with my early moral base and cultural environment, and who were the architects of my initial Mental Balance Sheet;

To my wife Donna, who is my best friend, partner, and who is a master at dealing with my somewhat turbulent entrepreneurial spirit; and

Most importantly, it is dedicated to the young students in our Fleischer Scholars Program in anticipation that it will provide an initial piece of the roadway needed for their personal development and success.

✶ Fleischer Scholars Primary Mission

I. To motivate qualified youngsters from the economically fragile sector to first get a college education and secondarily to emphasize and encourage a business education.

II. To provide a model and technique for learning how to think by:

    a. Understanding the 3-legged stool.

    b. The importance of goal setting and motivation.

    c. The importance of becoming a master adaptive learner.

III. To prepare scholars with techniques to acquire scholarships and graduate from college debt-free.

Foreword

Looking back on my life and career, I clearly see that there were some PIVOTAL moments in my life that put in place the basic mental framework which I used in my journey. The first was when I discovered the philosophic school of *EMPIRICISM*—we are a sum of all our personal experiences. The second and third were when I learned during my military service how a *GUIDED MISSILE* seeks out a target and combined that process with what I learned from reading *"Psycho Cybernetics."* I recognized my brain (when properly programmed) is a sophisticated computer-like, goal-seeking mechanism. This knowledge provided the basic framework which I used in learning, increasing my intellectual capital. establishing goals, and in business ventures. Combining them creates the **THREE-LEGGED STOOL** that my career and personal life is based upon.

This book is my attempt to explain and convey this process which was crucial in my becoming a Master Adaptive Learner and subsequently played an important part in my successes in life and business.

Marty Sheisher   3

Fleischer Scholars

**"Combining Knowledge
with a
Mind Roadmap
for
Success in Business and Life"**

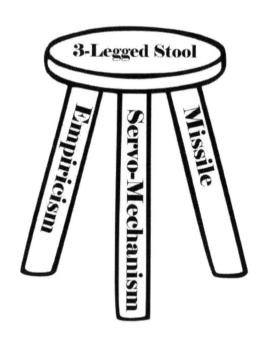

**to become a
Master Adaptive Learner**
www.fleischerscholars.com

The Fleischer Scholars Program combines knowledge with a mental roadmap for success in life and business, as pictorially illustrated by the 3-legged stool. The three legs of the stool represent 1) **Empiricism** -- you are a sum of all your personal experiences, 2) **Servo-mechanism** -- your brain is a sophisticated computer-like, goal-seeking mechanism, and 3) **Missile** -- you seek out a target and go towards that target. This mental roadmap encourages students to treat their brain like a computer, programming it throughout their lives (adapting as they learn) using the collection of their experiences and themselves as the missile to think more accurately and hit their target goals. Once Fleischer Scholar students understand how to use this mind roadmap, they can raise their personal thought process and level of intellectual capital, become master adaptive learners, successful leaders, and role models for their community.

A College Education Will Teach You to Become a Master Adaptive Learner

You Will Learn:
- How to *Learn*
- How to *Write*
- How to *Solve Problems*
- How to *Think*
- How to Be *Adaptable* and *Get Out of Your Comfort Zone!*

Table of Contents

Introducing Morton H. Fleischer

Currently, Mort Fleischer is a founder and Chairman of the Board of Directors of STORE Capital ("S|T|O|R|E") (NYSE: STOR), one of the largest, and certainly the fastest-growing net-lease Real Estate Investment Trust ("REIT") in the United States. Over nearly four decades, Mr. Fleischer has formed and managed more than twenty real estate companies, taking three of them public onto the New York Stock Exchange. These companies have successfully invested over $17 billion in single-tenant commercial real estate projects since 1981. Mr. Fleischer is an experienced financier, entrepreneur and real estate investor.

Prior to S|T|O|R|E Capital's formation, Mr. Fleischer co-founded Spirit Finance Corporation, also a REIT, and served as its Chairman from its inception in 2003 to February 2010, including the three years that Spirit Finance was publicly traded on the New York Stock Exchange—2004 to 2007. Mr. Fleischer founded seventeen other real estate limited partnerships in the 1980s and 1990s, which were predecessors and were merged to create Franchise Finance Corporation of America, a real estate investment trust that he formed and took public on the New York Stock Exchange in 1994. Mr. Fleischer served as FFCA's Chairman of the Board and Chief Executive Officer ("CEO") until it was acquired by GE Capital Corporation in 2001.

Mr. Fleischer received his Bachelor of Arts Degree from Washington University, St. Louis, Missouri, which awarded him its Distinguished Business Alumni Award in 1993.

Introduction

The Fleischer Scholars Program is Born

The Fleischer Scholars Program began as a summer bridge program in Arizona, which assists disadvantaged high school students (entering their senior year) interested in business careers, to make the transition into college. These "Fleischer Scholars" are provided a unique opportunity during a weeklong residential program (in Arizona, at the W. P. Carey School of Business at Arizona State University ("ASU")), to experience college life, and learn about entrepreneurship and business.

While I was initially searching for a university that could partner with the Fleischer Scholars Program and help fulfill my vision of providing a quality college education to students from economically fragile areas, who have the skills *and* desire to pursue business careers, it came to my attention that *Newsweek* magazine had called ASU the "most innovative university in America." I was surprised to find such a compatible university right in my own backyard. Upon my investigation, I realized that ASU was especially well suited to partner with the Fleischer Scholars Program and later on this was further substantiated after I read a book written by ASU's President, Michael

Crow, entitled *The New American Research University.* The Fleischer Scholars Program seeks to partner with specific types of universities, led by particular types of leaders, and as the Arizona State University Office of the President states on its website, Michael Crow is "... guiding the transformation of ASU into one of the nation's leading public metropolitan research universities, an institution that combines the highest levels of academic excellence, inclusiveness to a broad demographic, and maximum societal impact. The Fleischer Scholars Program is an important partner in supporting ASU's mission of measuring success by whom it *includes*, not by whom it *excludes*, and how those students succeed.

Over time, we plan on expanding the Fleischer Scholars Program to other universities and have already expanded our program to the Sam M. Walton College of Business at the University of Arkansas. They held their first Fleischer Scholars summer program in 2015 and have plans to continue our program every year. An agreement was entered into with the Olin Business School at Washington University in St. Louis to begin a Fleischer Scholars program which started in the summer of 2017 and has been successful and is continuing each year.

In 2018, the Thurgood Marshall College Fund (TMCF) announced the launch of the TMCF Fleischer HBCU Scholars program on three of their member universities: Fayetteville State University, Texas Southern University, and Virginia State University.

All Americans Should Be Included in the American Dream

I have always believed in my heart that we will never fully achieve the American dream unless our society creates ways to bring the socio-economically fragile people of this nation into the mainstream. I've come to understand that this wasn't going to just happen on its own, in a society as complex as ours, nor did I believe it could be accomplished by the American government's welfare system. So I set out on my own to assist in bringing the American Dream within the grasp of capable young people who don't normally understand the mechanisms of success and opportunity and how to achieve their goals.

My current attempt to find young people living in economically fragile circumstances, who possess the characteristics that will allow them to succeed, began with an idea that eventually evolved into the Fleischer Scholars Program. The inspiration came to me while I was on the campus of Washington University (my *alma mater*) in St. Louis, Missouri. High up in one of the university's buildings, as I looked out toward East St. Louis, Illinois, which is actually one of the most poverty stricken cities in the United States, I realized that there had to be a lot of smart and talented students out there, who "didn't know what they didn't know." I believed that if they were provided the right opportunities—like a college education—they could become responsible, productive citizens and make major contributions to the world that would otherwise go unrealized.

A Model for Fostering the Fleischer Scholars Program

In the past, I had first approached other universities with my idea and had varying degrees of success, but it was Bob Mittelstaedt, the Dean of ASU's W. P. Carey School of Business, who really understood and even shared my vision. I visited with Dean Mittelstaedt the day that my wife, Donna, and I donated our "Spirit" statue to the ASU business school. Bob was seated next to me at a dinner celebrating the donation of the "Spirit" statue which is discussed in Chapter 1 of this book, and as we talked, I shared my belief that to truly achieve the American dream, socio-economically fragile people had to be brought into the mainstream of society. When Bob told me that he was thinking the same thing and was willing to contribute the infrastructure and intellectual capital of ASU if I would contribute some "seed money," the partnership between the Fleischer Scholars Program and ASU was born. We both realized that many of the future leaders of America may reside in this underrepresented segment of society, and they need to be provided the educational opportunities that will help them to develop and succeed.

The Fleischer Scholars Bridge Program is a week-long summer program for high school students primarily between their junior and senior year, is free to its participants, and is tailored for economically disadvantaged high school students interested in pursuing business as a career and life-changing trajectory. Students selected for the program benefit from a multitude of resources, as they learn the necessary skills for success in college and beyond.

Fleischer Scholars Program students participate in the following:

- Life skills development—how to succeed and rise above socio-economic challenges

- Discovering academic and career opportunities in business

- Interacting with current students, faculty, staff, and alumni leading to successful relationships that can serve a lifetime

- Learning the keys to academic and professional success

- Applying for admission to college and learning about available financial assistance programs

- Receiving assistance after the Scholars Program throughout the college admission and enrollment process

Components of the program include

- Information about programs of study and corresponding careers

- Time management and college-level study skills

- Employer presentations

- Interaction and mentoring with current university students

- Faculty presentations and lectures

- Parent/guardian sessions

- Group projects and presentations

- On-site business visits

- Preparation for college: financial aid, scholarships and admission

- Instruction to professionalism and business etiquette

- Public speaking and effective presentation

Facilitators include:

- Selected university student leaders

- University and Business School academic advisors and student engagement and admissions staff

- Faculty

- Student Services representatives—mentors

- Business and industry representatives

In their final year of high school, participants in the Fleischer Scholars Program are contacted regularly, invited to business school and university events and programs, and supported throughout the college admissions and enrollment processes.

Qualification Criteria:

To qualify to participate in the program, students must:

- Come from an economically disadvantaged background;
- Achieve high test scores, *i.e.*, be intellectually qualified;
- Have the ability to deal with obstacles; and
- Be ambitious.

Since the first residential program in July 2010 and through the summer of 2016, the Fleischer Scholars Program has impacted over 650 students. Of those Scholars, an average of more than 75% have attended college.

In addition to our summer program, Fleischer Scholar attendees who can successfully "mine" scholarships that are available in the United States have a high potential to become college graduates, community leaders and role models. Through **Student Wallet**, a computer program designed by Fleischer Scholars graduate Josh Elizetxe, Fleischer Scholars is organizing and making access to the large, yet fragmented amount of scholarships available more accessible and efficient while simultaneously making the process of obtaining scholarships more "user-friendly". A ***debt free education*** is available to Fleischer Scholars without utilizing student loans as they access and use scholarships that are already available in the United States.

The Fleischer Scholars Program has changed lives and has done so with the commitment of each participating universities intellectual capital and infrastructure, our Fleischer Scholars success model, and an investment of love, understanding and other resources from my wife Donna, myself, and other contributors.

Morton H. Fleischer

CHAPTER ONE – THE FRAMEWORK THAT MAKES EVERYTHING POSSIBLE: LIVING IN AMERICA

The Unlimited Possibilities of America

One of the most powerful advantages in your life is the fact that you live in the United States of America. Within the framework of this great country, you can live and flourish. Unlike most other nations and societies of any age, America allows you to write the script of your own life! Our Founders formed a nation that allows all Americans to enjoy wide choices of opportunities—in a system of economic freedom, freedom of speech, and freedom of religion. As you appreciate the amazing environment for business opportunities this country affords you, you will need to develop your own capacity to succeed. Nobody will give you anything—you have to earn it. Those who sit around moping, waiting for someone to come along and give them what they want will be very sad throughout their entire lives—dissatisfied, unfulfilled, and even bitter. Understanding how to build something I have come to term your personal "Mental Balance Sheet," which we will begin to discuss in Chapter Two. In order to take control of and shape your own life, building your own personal Mental Balance Sheet is a fundamental head start, which should last a lifetime if you learn it well and take it seriously.

The Spirit Statue: A Symbol of American Freedom

The origin of the statue "Spirit" began in the late 1980s when my company developed a business park in Scottsdale, Arizona. We decided that we would like to commission a sculpture that would become a symbol of the economic and cultural environment that allows entrepreneurs and business people, like ourselves, to flourish in America, creating wealth and a higher standard of living for everyone.

Buck McCain, a well-known sculptor, painter and philosopher, created the "Spirit" sculpture combining the ideas that: America, represented by a democratic form of government which respects the rights of individuals to life, liberty and the pursuit of happiness; and a market driven economy, along with a cultural belief in the rule of law which strives for liberty and justice for all—creates high energy. He suggested the way to exemplify it was through a bronze sculpture that became known as "Spirit." The statue consists of five horses in motion, rising up out of the earth and it weighs 10,000 pounds. We believe that the horses artistically illustrate the power and creativity that is accomplished by combining America's political system, entrepreneurs, and business people. It is our symbol and has found a very appropriate home among students at a leading business school. The statue is surrounded by four plaques, which highlight the philosophy and ideals that inspired the creation of Spirit. The first plaque attributes the creation of the statue to Buck McCain in 1987, and notes that it was given as a gift to Arizona State University by Mort and Donna Fleischer of Scottsdale, Arizona in 2009. As stated on the second of the four plaques surrounding the statue:

> "Spirit symbolizes the power of freedom in America. It is the combination of political and economic freedom that creates democratic capitalism, which makes up the economic and cultural environment of America. This system combines an incentive-driven market economy, a strong legal framework that values individual property rights, a representative government that respects the rights of individuals to life, liberty, and the pursuit of happiness, and a system of cultural institutions moved by the principles of liberty and justice for all. These converging ideas provide Americans with unlimited possibilities for economic success and the freedom to voluntarily contribute to our society, thus creating more opportunities for succeeding generations."

The third of the four plaques around "Spirit" further elucidates the philosophy and ideas that the statue represents:

> "Art and philosophy have the power to inspire and impact our lives. Spirit reminds us that in a free society there are no limits on the creative possibilities of our ideas. The horses, which rise up from the earth, reflect the indomitable spirit of America and the boundless opportunities freedom affords us. Art and philosophy provide us with symbolism and intellectual guidance. Through freedom we have the opportunity to shape ourselves into the men and women we hope to become."

The statement on the fourth of the plaques surrounding the statue is an inspiration to all who read it, and especially to future businessmen and women:

In *America* the Only Limits to

What You Will Be Able to Achieve Are

Your Own Courage and Talent.

SPIRIT BY BUCK McCAIN

In America, You Determine Your Own Future

The combination of political and economic freedom that exists in America is the basis of the economic and cultural environment of this country. Americans have unlimited possibilities for economic success and the freedom to voluntarily contribute to our society, thus "writing the scripts for their own lives," and creating more opportunities for succeeding generations. You can make a difference in this world for yourself and for others! You can leave it a better place than you found it.

In America, your future is not determined by your past or your present circumstances. **Your future is determined *by you*, and it starts *now*.**

CHAPTER TWO – BUILDING YOUR PERSONAL WEALTH: DEVELOPING YOUR MENTAL BALANCE SHEET

You Are Who You Are Becoming!

What kind of future do you want? Do you want to have happiness, income, wealth, and success? Do you want to "write the script of your own life?" Would you like to "make a difference" in this world? Do you want your life's journey to be rewarding and exciting? Or is it your vision to continue living in the same neighborhood where you grew up, pursuing a mundane and probably unfulfilling career?

Each of us comes to this world with our own unique gifts, abilities, talents, and personalities. *These are your assets*. They are *yours alone*, and they make you the *unique individual that you are*. If you use your assets appropriately, they will assist in providing you with a permanent source of happiness, income, wealth and success. Most importantly, your assets will provide you the foundation to have a fulfilling, rewarding and exciting life's journey. Your sojourn on this planet is for only a limited amount of time, yet you have the ability to make a contribution and therefore make a difference.

Your ability to improve the world at large, your personal world, and your future life, all depend on what you do with your unique assets. If you use them properly, you can achieve anything! Get out a piece of paper—right now—and make a list of your assets. This list is part of what I like to call your personal "Mental Balance Sheet." Just as a business has a financial balance sheet—a list of all the assets, liabilities and equity of a company—we, as people, each have our own individual Mental Balance Sheet.

The following is a very basic example of a business financial balance sheet:

XYZ COMPANY
Balance Sheet
December 31, 2018

ASSETS	LIABILITIES & OWNER'S EQUITY
Current assets	Current liabilities
Investments	Long-term liabilities
Land, buildings and equipment	Total liabilities
Intangible assets	Owner's equity
Other assets	
Total assets	

Review the following example of what a personal Mental Balance Sheet *can* look like. Notice that "John Smith's" assets fall into three main classifications: Intellectual Capital, such as knowledge derived from formal education; Empirical Knowledge, which includes all that he learns from his life experiences; and Moral Compass assets, which include his moral values and aspects of his personal character.

Also notice that "John Smith" has some liabilities, which could impede his possibilities for success:

JOHN SMITH
Mental Balance Sheet
January 1, 2019

ASSETS	LIABILITIES
Intellectual Capital	Lacks advanced (college) education
Intelligence	
Academic Knowledge	Sometimes repeats his mistakes
	Has a powerful fear of failure
	Negative attitude
Empirical Knowledge	Fails to stay focused
Learns from experience	Spends too much time with people of low character
Strong social skills	
Ambitious	
Moral Compass	
Strong moral values	

Your Mental Balance Sheet guides how you think and is built on your education, knowledge and experience, which give you *power*. It determines how your mind operates when you're learning, when you're overcoming your weaknesses, and when you're making decisions and achieving goals. It is your personal wealth, which is *yours alone*. **Knowledge is a powerful asset.** You can continue to acquire knowledge through personal experience, formal education *and* by reading uplifting, wisdom-building, educational books (as I discovered when I read, amongst others, Maxwell Maltz' powerful book, *Psycho-Cybernetics.*)

New experiences can also be an impactful and powerful tool for adding assets to your Mental Balance Sheet. Empiricism is the concept that much of our knowledge derives from our personal experiences and we are a sum of them. Consider the example of a young baby who has always been well cared for by his Mother. She meets all of his needs as they arise, and he has developed trust. One day the baby is sitting on the floor of a daycare center enjoying a lollipop, when another baby crawls over to him and steals it. He immediately learns that you can't always trust others! This is an example of empiricism—acquiring new knowledge through personal experience.

As you acquire intellectual knowledge (Intellectual Capital) and have more experiences (growth through empiricism or your own personal experience), eventually you will be able to manufacture new knowledge, *i.e.*, be able to recognize opportunities and learn new ways to take advantage of the opportunities you see. **Understanding how to continue building the assets of your Mental Balance Sheet in order to shape your own life** is a fundamental strategy that can last you a lifetime. Participating in the Fleischer Scholars Program is a first step toward achieving this goal.

Many of the assets on my Mental Balance Sheet are derived from my college education, military service, and the multiple businesses in which I engaged over the course of my career. I do not consider those business endeavors as "jobs," rather, they were learning experiences from which I **gained assets** for my **Mental Balance Sheet**, and they helped me to **accomplish my ultimate goal of building a company to my design**. From each of those business opportunities I acquired knowledge, experience and skills that added assets to my Mental Balance Sheet. As my story unfolds in these pages we will discuss my multiple business pursuits, and how I was able to add assets to my personal Mental Balance Sheet gained from each of them which eventually allowed me to define my ultimate goal of building a company to my design. I want to share these experiences with you in the hope that they will PROVIDE YOU WITH A TECHNIQUE that will assist you in pursuing a successful life's journey.

Start thinking about your personal Mental Balance Sheet. At the end of this chapter I have provided you with a blank form for your own Mental Balance Sheet. Make a copy of it, and as we continue our discussion in this book about my experiences, follow along with me by filling in that blank Mental Balance Sheet with the assets you come to recognize that I gained during my experiences, along with any liabilities you recognize I acquired from my college education, years of military service, and the varied business endeavors in which I engaged. At various places in my story you will have the opportunity to compare your answers with my own version of my Mental Balance Sheet, which will contain my assessments of the assets I gained and the liabilities I acquired from my education, military and business experiences. By completing the blank Mental Balance Sheet as you read this book, you will develop the crucial skill of being able to recognize and understand the assets and liabilities that derive from our life experiences.

As I acknowledged earlier, my Mother and Father were the initial architects of my Mental Balance Sheet, although my early life and jobs all contributed to its development. My ancestors had been butchers in Austria. In fact, the name "Fleischer" derives from their profession: "Fleisch" means "meat" in German. My Father's family emigrated to the U.S. from Austria in 1898, when he was just six months old. They moved to Omaha, Nebraska, which was a major cattle center in the U.S.—where else would a family of butchers want to go? After my Father grew up and married my Mother, who was born in the U.S., they moved to Texas. I was born in 1936 in Dallas, Texas, near the end of the Great Depression. A few years later, in Cameron, Texas, my family entered the retail business. My parents moved shortly thereafter to Litchfield, Illinois, a small town where my Father and Mother opened a ladies ready-to-wear retail store in 1940.

My parents put me to work, and kept me busy. Even my early jobs as a young boy contributed to the development of my Mental Balance Sheet. I started out mowing lawns: first with a manual push mower, then after a time I borrowed money and bought a power mower. Mowing with the push mower was a lot of work, and I thought to myself, "There must be a better way to do this!" I realized I could mow more lawns, and make more money, using a power mower. So I borrowed the money to enable my investment in the power mower, and the increased income from being able to mow more lawns more than paid for it. That was my first experience in capital investment, and in using leverage (debt) to increase my profits, both of which were great business lessons. This new knowledge became assets for my Mental Balance Sheet.

When I was old enough, I worked as a janitor in the family store after school. My responsibilities included sweeping, dusting, and washing windows. Due to the onset of winter, there were no lawns to mow and I was running out of money. With the janitorial experience that I had gained working in the family store, I got a job as a janitor in a Woolworth dime store. In the attic above that store was the most horrible mess I had ever seen! I took it upon myself to clean it up. I wasn't asked to do it—I just decided to do it, because it needed doing. When my boss saw what I had accomplished, he was very excited! He told me I had done a really good job, and even called my Father and told him. My Father was so proud of me! All of that praise resulted in me being proud of me! Through that experience I began to learn the joy of achievement, which is a permanent motivator and a great asset for my Mental Balance Sheet. That early position also taught me how to be responsible, how to take initiative, and I began to understand how small business organizations function (three more assets for my Mental Balance Sheet).

Take this opportunity to complete the adjacent blank Mental Balance Sheet, fill in the assets I gained and liabilities I acquired based on what you have read thus far about my life and experiences.

MR. FLEISCHER'S
Early Mental Balance Sheet
1949-1952

<u>ASSETS</u>   <u>LIABILITIES</u>

Empirical Knowledge/ Personal Experience

_____

_____

_____

Intellectual Capital

_____

_____

_____

Moral Compass

_____

_____

As previously mentioned, one of the main purposes of this book is to help you understand how to build your own Mental Balance Sheet by illustrating the example of how I built mine. As you know, **all new knowledge and new experiences (empiricism) add assets (or liabilities)** to your Mental Balance Sheet. It is my hope that you will learn for yourself how to recognize and utilize the assets you gain from your own experiences to form goals, to reach your goals, and to enhance your life.

Compare the assets and liabilities you wrote in the blank Mental Balance Sheet (above) with the assets and liabilities I noted myself for my Early Mental Balance Sheet:

MR. FLEISCHER'S
EARLY MENTAL BALANCE SHEET
1949-1953

ASSETS	LIABILITIES
Empirical Knowledge	I didn't know what I didn't know
	Small world view

- Loving and supportive parents
- "Huck Finn" type environment:
    - hunting-fishing-swimming in creeks
- Ran my first business (lawn mowing)
    - Introduction to use of leverage and capital investment to increase profits
    - Beginning to understand the joy of achievement
- Benefits of taking initiative

Intellectual Capital
- Public school education

Moral Compass
- Traditional Judeo-Christian values
- Strong American mid-western values and work ethics

Using the blank balance sheet below, build *your* own Mental Balance Sheet using your:

- Empirical Knowledge/Personal Experience
- Intellectual Capital
- Moral Compass

ASSETS   LIABILITIES

Empirical Knowledge/ Personal Experience

_____

_____

_____

Intellectual Capital

_____

_____

_____

Moral Compass

_____

CHAPTER THREE – BECOMING A MASTER ADAPTIVE LEARNER

Empiricism: You Are the Sum of All of Your Experiences

Our world is constantly changing, and the way you deal with that either becomes an asset (if you are forward-thinking and make adjustments) or a liability (if you don't make adjustments and are "left behind" by your peers and the rest of the world).

Adaptive learning means learning from feedback and positive (or negative) reinforcement. Consider the examples of how Amazon.com markets its products to you, as a consumer. When you first sign up for this Internet-based service, it offers a very generic, basic group of products that the site suggests for you to purchase. Later, based on how you respond to those products and what you actually buy, the site starts making more and more suggestions, which are unique to you. This is how Amazon.com learns about you as a consumer, adapting its sales pitch as it fills in its balance sheet about you.

Why is it important to become a MASTER ADAPTIVE LEARNER? Because our world is constantly changing, and if anything, the speed of that change is going to continue to increase during your lifetime. If you want to live a successful life, you need to have **a mindset of continuous learning**; you need to be able to **respond to your**

changing environment. You will need to continue to learn for your entire life. Perhaps a good illustration of a business that failed because its leaders did not recognize and respond to its changing environment is the stunning case of Blockbuster Video. The first Blockbuster Video store was opened in Dallas, Texas in 1985. Its business grew quickly, and by 1992 the company was the leading provider of video rentals, with over 2,800 stores operating around the world. In 1997, Silicon Valley veteran Reed Hastings founded Netflix, partly out of frustration because he was charged $40 in late fees by Blockbuster for returning a video late. Netflix grew quickly and became a publicly owned company in 2002. By 2004, Blockbuster was at its peak, with over 9,000 stores worldwide. Just six short years later, in September 2010, Blockbuster filed for bankruptcy protection, with a goal to wipe out about $1 billion in debt. DISH Network bought the assets of Blockbuster at auction in 2011, and in 2012 Dish announced plans to begin closing more than 1,700 Blockbuster retail locations in the U.S. In 2013, it was announced that the remaining U.S. stores would be closed.[1]

How did such a mammoth enterprise fail so completely in such a relatively short amount of time? Blockbuster's management apparently failed to recognize that the Netflix business model held much greater appeal for consumers. There were many indications that this was the case, but Blockbuster ignored them all. Times had changed and consumer buying trends were different: people preferred to have their DVDs delivered to their door via the mail, rather than having to leave home to rent a movie. Blockbuster's pricing model failed to change as competition made renting cheaper for the consumer, and the late-night runs to the local Blockbuster store to avoid late fees made Blockbuster an inconvenient choice. Blockbuster's vast real estate holdings were a significant drain on the company's resources, while in comparison, Netflix had very little overhead. Blockbuster could not compete, and that huge company failed. This story of Blockbuster's failure illustrates other important principles, which we discuss in more detail at a later point. They are: (1) it is critical to know your competition; and (2) it is critical to add value to both your customers and shareholders.

We all must learn these lessons. My own personal lesson that the world is constantly changing was learned in a very harsh way during my first two years of high school, when both of my parents passed away. My Mother died when I was just 14, during my freshman year in high school, of brain cancer. My Father died about 18 months later—of a disease I call heartbreak. It was really emotionally harmful to me to lose both of my parents, so close together, at such a young age. I was confused and felt adrift in life. My sister and I moved in with an aunt and uncle in St. Louis. That was a huge change and a major culture shock for me. Moving from rural Litchfield, Illinois, where I had had an idyllic "Huck Finn" type of childhood—hunting, fishing, and swimming in creeks—to the "concrete jungle" of St. Louis, was a difficult and dramatic change. I was suddenly thrust into a lower-middle class school named "Soldan High School." I found myself in a faster-paced city environment with a lot of smart aleck kids who had grown up in a completely different culture. When I reminisced about my childhood pleasures, like fishing and swimming in creeks, they ridiculed me, and said I was a yokel, and treated me with contempt. In fact, I *was* a yokel—because I didn't know what I didn't know, and I didn't realize the whole world hadn't grown up and didn't live the way I had in Litchfield. My life experiences —"empiricism"—were quite limited. In addition to grieving the loss of my parents, I was suddenly and involuntarily transplanted to a completely foreign world of insensitive city kids with whom I seemed to have nothing in common. We moved to a different neighborhood and I transferred to University High School, from which I graduated.

Intellectual Capital: Education is a Valuable Asset!

I was fortunate in that my family placed strong emphasis on the importance of a college education. My sister was a diabetic, and my aunt and uncle suggested that I needed to stay close by to help take care of her. Washington University is a fine institution and was right there in St. Louis. They thought I should enroll there, and I agreed, so I attended college at Washington University.

At Washington University, I again experienced the huge cultural difference between my background and the kids in the fraternity I joined, Pi Lambda Phi. To all the "city kids" in the fraternity, I was a "country" boy, because of my background. They nicknamed me "Bumpkin." It was a mean nickname that was hurtful and debilitating. I desperately missed my parents and my happy childhood environment. Finding myself in another foreign and uncomfortable situation, I felt alone and very lost—without a rudder to steer me or a counselor to guide me. I suffered from low self-esteem and bit my nails unconsciously because of the enormous stress. It absolutely devastated me, and I wasn't as good of a student as I might have been in a better emotional environment.

Despite my frustrations and obstacles, I wanted to gain a good college education. As I pursued my college studies, instinctively I believed I should have a broad worldview, so I studied both liberal arts and business courses. I learned some worldly and business basics through the combination of studying humanities, philosophy, and business subjects. I still remember my first day studying an elementary logic question: "If A equals B, and B equals C, then what is A?" The answer, of course, is that "A" equals "C." This class was enormously helpful in teaching me how to think and reason logically. It provided a structured framework to my thinking that had been absent most of my life. My philosophy courses also left a strong impression on me. What I didn't know at the time was that I was beginning to learn the underlying framework on which the modern world is built, and the philosophic basis upon which it relies. I began to recognize that I was gaining the basic assets for my Mental Balance Sheet. I was learning how to **think, communicate, write and solve problems**, which are the primary reasons for attending college. I had the privilege of being exposed to great ideas, such as empiricism, and the ideas of many great philosophers which I read while in college or later in life, including:

- Thomas Hobbes (who expressed the idea of a nation-state with a social contract between the ruler and the ruled);
- Adam Smith (who taught his theories of the "invisible hand" that regulates markets);
- John Stuart Mill (a proponent of liberty; the founder of a capitalist state, free trade, intellectual freedom and advocate for less state interference in business endeavors);
- Karl Marx (who promoted principles of common ownership, communism); and
- Sidney and Beatrice Webb (who were powerful advocates for socialism in Britain).

My classes also exposed me to the philosophies of:

- Renowned economist John Maynard Keynes (he combined the concepts of capitalism, big government spending and regulation, and we continue to be influenced by his theories called "Keynesian Economics");

- Theodore Roosevelt (a "lion-tamer" to Laissez Faire (or unregulated) capitalism, a regulator and a trust-buster);

- Francis Bacon (famous for his philosophy that "knowledge is power");

- René Descartes (promoted the idea that "I think, therefore I am"); and

- Joseph Schumpeter (who invented the term "Creative Destruction" in describing how new capitalistic methods of production and finance destroy older, less efficient ones).

The subjects I studied in college had a huge impact on me. They added substantially to my Mental Balance Sheet because I increased my Intellectual Capital by adding knowledge, and my classes and other college life experiences also added assets to my Empirical Knowledge as I gained a broader worldview. I was beginning to learn the framework of how the modern world works. It started me on the road to thinking about how to develop what I now call my "Mental Balance Sheet" *assets*.

I remember with particular fondness my philosophy class with Professor Huston Smith, titled "Religions of the East and West." Professor Smith was the son of a Christian missionary Father and a

Chinese Mother. He was six feet four inches tall, with Asian eyes. Professor Smith was a luminary; he had written books on eastern and western religions, including Judaism, Daoism, Hinduism, Buddhism, all the branches of Christianity, and Sanskrit. I studied all kinds of religions in his class. I learned a lot, including that the moral base is pretty much the same through all of these religions and world philosophies. Their practitioners are all trying to get to the same place—more or less. He gave us a broad view of most of the major religions and some of the smaller religions in the world, which was helpful to my young mind.

While pursuing my education, I also studied history, finance, English, accounting, geology, statistics, marketing and advertising. I realized that one goes to college to learn **how to learn**, **how to write**, **how to solve problems**, and **how to be adaptable**—and continually get out of your comfort zone.

I began to develop a rudder as I acquired knowledge, and it became clear to me that I needed to have **a mindset geared toward continuous learning.** Knowledge—a major part of your Intellectual Capital—is a critically important asset for your Mental Balance Sheet.

Becoming a Master Adaptive Learner

It gradually dawned on me, and it is much clearer these many years later, that the pace of increasing knowledge and change is getting faster and faster with each passing year. The recorded history of man in the modern world is roughly 6,000 years, yet the first ideas of a nation state (as advocated by Thomas Hobbes) only began to appear in 1650. And the evolving world as we know it really didn't begin until the mid-1800s, with economic thinkers such as Adam Smith and John Stuart Mill, who lived during the industrial revolution. In relation to the recorded history of man, the world has moved at "light speed" since those times. For the student reading this book, the pace of increasing knowledge and change will move *ever faster* during your career. It is a critical skill (and asset for your Mental Balance Sheet) that you are able to adapt as the world around you changes.

My new knowledge helped me begin to **overcome my weaknesses**, and not realizing it, I was becoming a MASTER ADAPTIVE LEARNER as I developed some initial knowledge of the world and augmented my Mental Balance Sheet with assets of knowledge and experience that I could use to develop a career. **A college education can provide the foundation and framework to help *you* become a Master Adaptive Learner and live your life as a continuous learner, which is what I have done. My college education has helped me immensely.** Because the world is constantly changing, and it is impossible to predict the future, becoming a Master Adaptive Learner is an important key to living a successful life, and is critical to ensure you are best prepared for a career in business and life. As a Master Adaptive Learner, you will possess the tools to adapt your thinking (and your business practices) as the world changes.

My college education and experiences also helped me to recognize the importance of **MOTIVATION** and **CHARACTER** while working toward my goals, and I realized the need to constantly readjust those goals higher as my knowledge increased. This thought process was continually reinforced as I became aware that many successful Americans come from very humble beginnings.

You Don't Know What You Don't Know

The more our world changes, the more complicated it becomes. You need to be very aware of the fact that you don't know what you don't know. Take a moment and think about that statement. You don't know what you don't know. Some say that ignorance is bliss—which means that if you don't know what's going on around you, you aren't anxious about the potential hazards. You also aren't aware of the potential opportunities, however, or the great experiences that could be had with a little effort on your part. In fact, you just don't know what you don't know. The more you experience in life, and the more education you acquire, the more you will realize there are an almost infinite number of things you don't know. The more you know, the better you understand this.

Consider each new experience you undergo in life as adding assets to your personal Mental Balance Sheet. We are the sum of all of our experiences (empiricism). The more we experience, the more we learn, and therefore, the more assets we gain for our Mental Balance

Sheets. Any new knowledge you acquire also adds assets to your Mental Balance Sheet. As your knowledge assets (your Intellectual Capital and Empirical Knowledge) broaden, your goals will become clearer and better defined. You should also become skilled at dispelling non-productive beliefs, which cause unnecessary and wasteful distractions. Eventually, you will be able to acquire new knowledge (assets) that constitutes new ways to become aware of and take advantage of opportunities you begin to see.

Liabilities on a Mental Balance Sheet

Just as your experiences can add assets to your Mental Balance Sheet, experiences can also add liabilities to your Mental Balance Sheet, if you let them (i.e., if you don't learn from them). Failure to set goals, making unclear goals, fear of failure, self-pity or blaming others, emotional baggage such as prejudices and your own ineptitude, all constitute liabilities on your Mental Balance Sheet. Negative thought processes will result in too many liabilities on your Mental Balance Sheet, all of which will cause your brain to send the wrong thoughts and impede positive, successful results.

A Positive Self-Image: An Important Asset

You should include in the assets of your personal Mental Balance Sheet a positive self-image. If you don't feel like you currently have a positive self-image, you can take steps to correct that, to see yourself more accurately.

Consider the following excerpt from *Psycho-Cybernetics*:

Get a New Mental Picture of Yourself

The unhappy, failure-type personality cannot develop a new self-image by pure will power, or by arbitrarily deciding to. There must be some grounds, some justification, some reason for deciding that the old picture of self is in error, and that a new picture is appropriate. You cannot merely imagine a new self-image; unless you feel that it is based upon *truth*. Experience has shown that when a person does change his self-image, he has the feeling that for one reason or another, he "sees," or realizes the truth about himself.

* * *

Science has now confirmed what philosophers, mystics, and other intuitive people have long declared: every human being has been literally "engineered for success" by his Creator. Every human being has access to a power greater than himself.

This means "YOU." As Emerson has said, "There are no great and no small."

If you were engineered for success and happiness, then the old picture of yourself as unworthy of happiness, of a person who was "meant" to fail, must be in error.[2]

If you do not believe that you currently have a positive self-image, it is time to change that. You have a powerful basis and justification for adopting a new, positive self-image: the fact that you are one of a very few, elite students who were invited to participate further in the Fleischer Scholars Program, for example. That you are reading this book, and possibly selected to further participate in the Fleischer Scholars Program is itself evidence that you are an intelligent, ambitious, confident person with a goal of furthering your education by attending college, and a long-term goal of pursuing a career in business. Remember that you were "engineered for success and happiness," and you deserve to be successful and happy.

To get there, it is important for you to have a positive self-image, because as noted in *Psycho-Cybernetics*, "You act, and feel, not according to what things are really like, but according to the image your mind holds of what they are like."[3] Let's think about our perception of reality for just a moment. You may feel like you come from an undesirable background. Remember how I was thought of as a bumpkin? What are you? Has anyone ever referred to you as something you didn't like? Very few people are born into wealth—so do you think of yourself as poor? If so, is it a true belief? You need to change the way you see yourself, and your life. You are surrounded by opportunities. You are privileged, compared with the rest of the world, and almost every human that lived on the earth before you. You live in America! Get your head straight about this. Get a better self-image fixed in your head, and realize how rich your life is and how many opportunities are yours if you will just look up and avail yourself of them.

It is important to set clear goals, remain focused on your goals, and not be distracted by information that will not help you reach your goals—what I call the lies, emotional baggage and the "minutiae" of life, which would constitute another liability on your Mental Balance Sheet.

Fear of Failure

Do not be afraid to fail! A person is not failing when he attempts to execute ideas—rather, he is **learning**. You need to be a MASTER ADAPTIVE LEARNER. There is no success without failure. Can you ride a bike? Could you always ride a bike? Do you recall how you were frozen with fear before you learned, and then you tried and failed a few times, only to fill your life with the freedom to zip around at high speeds when you finally developed the skill to ride the bicycle? What if you had never confronted that false fear, had never tried and failed a few times, and had never learned to ride? Where would you be now? Do not clutter your mind with the fear of failure. It has been said that, "A head full of fears has no space for dreams" (author unknown). There is reason for apprehension, because the pace at which man is increasing his knowledge is growing at a mind-boggling pace:

"Buckminster Fuller created the "Knowledge Doubling Curve"; he noticed that until 1900 human knowledge doubled approximately every century. By the end of World War II knowledge was doubling every 25 years. Today things are not as simple as different types of knowledge have different rates of growth. For example, nanotechnology knowledge is doubling every two years and clinical knowledge every 18 months. But on average, human knowledge is doubling every 13 months. According to IBM, the build out of the "internet of things" will lead to the doubling of knowledge every 12 hours.[4]

The world is moving so much faster now, it is crucial to be a MASTER ADAPTIVE LEARNER, which will enable you to succeed in life and in business.

Learning to Trust Your Instincts

I mentioned that as I studied at Washington University, I became acquainted with the concept of empiricism: "You are the sum of all of your experiences." The more you learn from your experiences as you journey through life, the more developed your instincts (which I believe are honed by how you program your subconscious mind and is your subconscious mind at work) become. It is a wise practice always to trust your instincts, especially when they are based on your moral compass, which we will discuss in the next chapter. If something deep inside you gives you the feeling that something is not right about a person or situation, trust it. It is probably your subconscious mind cautioning you. If your instincts are well-developed, they will generally not lead you astray.

Take this opportunity to again fill in the assets (and liabilities) on the blank Mental Balance Sheet that you recognize I gained from my college experiences. Then compare what you wrote with the example of my post-college Mental Balance Sheet (below). By the time I completed my college education, as you can see from the Mental Balance Sheet below my assets had grown substantially in all three asset classifications: Empirical Knowledge, Intellectual Capital, and Moral Compass Assets.

ADDITIONS TO MR. FLEISCHER'S
MENTAL BALANCE SHEET
1954-1958 (College years)

ASSETS	LIABILITIES
Empirical Knowledge:	I *still* didn't know what I didn't know

- Learning to become an Adaptive Master Learner

Intellectual Capital:
- Studied
  - Philosophy
  - Economics
  - Business Subjects
  - English
  - History
- I learned
  - How to learn
  - How to write
  - How to solve problems

- How to think
- How to be adaptable and get
  out of my comfort zone

Moral Compass:
- I learned the detrimental impact of unkind people

CHAPTER NOTES

[1]Phillips, Matt and Ferdman, Roberto A. "Wow, What a Difference: a Brief, Illustrated History of Blockbuster, Which is Closing the Last of its U.S. Stores", November 6, 2013. www.qz.com. Accessed November 25, 2015.

[2]Maltz, Dr. Maxwell. *Psycho-Cybernetics.* Simon & Schuster, New York. 1960. pp. 27-28.

[3]*Ibid.,* p.34.

[4]Schilling, David Russell. *Industry Tap Into News.* "Knowledge Doubling Every 12 Months, Soon to be Every 12 Hours." www.industrytap.com. Accessed January 23, 2016.

CHAPTER FOUR – YOUR MORAL COMPASS: A CRUCIAL ASSET

When I asked you to make a list of your assets in Chapter Two, did you include your moral compass—your values? If you didn't, add it to the list now. Your moral compass is a crucial group of assets in your life, and they should appear on your Mental Balance Sheet. It doesn't matter whether or not you were raised within an organized religion—you have a moral compass. I did not grow up attending worship services every week. My family is Jewish, and my parents taught me the basics; I was even bar mitzvah'd, although I dreaded the experience. But I had that foundation—taught right from wrong, and to treat others well, along with the principles which form America's Judeo-Christian culture. You may recall that I mentioned that during my early years I grew up in a "Tom Sawyer – Huck Finn" type of environment...we were "free spirits." That upbringing was based on traditional Judeo-Christian and strong mid-western moral values, and they contributed significantly to the building of my personal moral compass. I learned that a person's word is his bond. My parents were a great example to me. My Father especially placed a lot of trust in people. I remember hearing my parents discussing customers who owed money to their retail business, but were slow to pay, and my Father would reassure my Mother, "Don't worry Rose, they are our friends and they will pay us." Most of their customers were farmers and coal miners. Times were tough and their financial circumstances were often challenging. But my Father always had faith in them and trusted they would pay their bills, and for the most part, they did.

I believe that the Judeo-Christian value structure, along with others that are similar, is an integral part of our cultural heritage. It's what holds America together, because we all come from different places, believe in different religions, and have different backgrounds, yet in my opinion, we all get along fairly well. When I studied philosophy in college, I began to understand that every country has a cultural heritage, and I have come to believe that America's is the best. The nation's foundation was constructed from what the Founding Fathers purposefully laid down—it did not happen randomly. America is full of people who embrace the "Protestant ethic" and work hard, and that culture, together with the framework of our laws created by our Founders, combined with our country's values, result in our cultural heritage and economic success.

One of the great blessings and advantages of living in America is that our laws are based on high moral values: Judeo-Christian moral values. You don't need to seek out religion or a particular church to be knowledgeable about those values; they are the foundation of our laws.

Be of Strong Character

You need look no further than the 10 Commandments that Moses (in the Old Testament) brought down from the mountain to the Children of Israel to lay a solid foundation for your moral compass: "thou shalt not steal," and "thou shalt not kill," to name just two of the commandments. Couple that with the age-old principle that we should treat others in the same way that we ourselves want to be treated, and it isn't hard to figure out the appropriate course of action in pretty much any situation.

An important strategy is to *decide ahead of time how you will choose to act.* Draw a circle around the things that you will, and those you will not do. If you plan in advance, it will be much easier to know how you should act when a challenge arises, because you will have already decided. You won't have to think about it. And the more you rely upon and follow your moral compass, the stronger it will become.

I learned from my Father's experience that good people want to do what's right. Surround yourself with good people. Don't surround yourself with people of bad character. It is *critical* to your success in life that you work with and deal with intelligent, high-quality, high-character, trustworthy people of integrity. Work with people who are highly motivated. As Abraham Lincoln said "Stand with a man when he is morally right and leave him when he goes wrong."

During my business career I had more than one occasion to deal with people of questionable morals. The results were never good. While operating a coal mine in Birmingham, Alabama, some Alabama "good ol' boys" attempted at one point to extort bribery money from my company. The coal mine had only two customers: Alabama Power and U.S. Steel. One afternoon, two men from Alabama Power walked into my office and announced that if I did not pay money to them personally (*i.e.*, pay them "kickbacks" or bribes), Alabama Power would not buy any more coal from my company. Their demands amounted to extortion, of course, and I was not about to comply. I kicked them out of my office, and the end result was that it was no longer wise for me to do business in Birmingham, Alabama. Ultimately, both of those men ended up in jail after a Grand Jury Investigation, at which I testified and learned that America's judicial system works. But in the meantime, I saved my company a lot of money, and I avoided any future attempts at a "shake-down" because I didn't accede to their demands, and most importantly, I stuck to my moral compass.

I also learned while in the coal mining business that people of suspect character do not honor their contracts. The miners and truck drivers were organized into two labor unions: the United Mine Workers (UMW) and the Teamsters Union. Before long, it became clear that if the unions did not like their contracts, they did not honor them. I might as well not have made the contracts. The end result for my company was that we didn't get the benefit of the deals we thought we had made.

Wall Street: Where Money, Wisdom and Knowledge Meet Greed and Avarice

When I was in the mergers and acquisitions business, Wall Street acted as a powerful "schoolroom" for me with regard to the difference in dealing with wise, honest people and doing business with people of low moral character. The people of high character are the people who generally succeed over the long term. Financial giant E. F. Hutton (which for a time financed one of my business ventures) eventually failed because of the short-term and improper vision, greed and avarice of some of its corporate leaders. This caused severe financial difficulties for them and they were eventually taken over by another firm.

I had some disappointing experiences dealing with Wall Street bankers, especially during the early years of my career. I never knew when I called on them whether they would be my partner and finance my venture, or steal my business idea. I learned that at some levels, agreements needed to be memorialized in writing and a "good old-fashioned Midwestern handshake" wasn't enough for some people to honor their commitments. A couple of examples are as follows: as you'll see in later chapters, my goal of building a company revolved around what we label "Single-tenant" real estate. In my early days in this business I called on Lehman Brothers (an investment bank which is now bankrupt and no longer in existence) and Metropolitan Life Insurance Company, asking them to invest funds. Both companies took my ideas and went into the business themselves, becoming my competitors. From this experience, I learned that confidentiality and non-compete agreements were critically important.

Your Reputation—A Priceless Asset

It was also Wall Street that taught me the value of having a good reputation. During the 1980s when I was raising money through public limited partnerships in my Single-tenant Real Estate Finance business, there was one occasion when I was talking to a room full (300-400) of investors. It was a big group of people. As I informed our investors that the limited partnership hadn't been financially successful enough that year to enable us to meet our yield commitment to them (the minimum cash distributions we had committed that the investors would receive), people were clearly disappointed and unhappy—until I informed them that I was going to meet our yield commitment anyway, by taking from our own fees the funds that were lacking. In other words, I was going to make up the difference to the investors by taking it out of my share of the earnings from the limited partnership. Needless to say, the mood in the room changed instantaneously. After the meeting, many of the investors approached me to shake my hand, and two or three people from Wall Street even walked up to me and said, "It's nice to know you,

Mort! There aren't a lot of moral men on Wall Street." At the time of re-writing this book, I am 82 years old, and when I go to Wall Street, many people are still glad to see me. It often doesn't take much to set yourself apart, and make yourself memorable. Integrity is often that difference. In fact, it is one of the main human characteristics that our economic system relies upon for its success.

I recall one occasion recently when I was on Wall Street with a securities offering, and I had to tell a prospective investor that I didn't have any business cards with me. His immediate response was, "Don't worry, Mort. We don't need any cards. We know who you are." Having a good reputation is irreplaceable. Never jeopardize your good reputation by acting contrary to your moral compass. Your reputation is one of the most priceless assets of your Mental Balance Sheet, for all of your life. It can take a lifetime to build a good reputation, which can quickly and easily be destroyed. Never trade the value of your lifelong reputation for a quick profit. Thankfully, it was early in my career that I learned the incredible value of a good reputation.

Never Deviate From Your Moral Compass

In the 1960s when I operated an upscale retail men's clothing store in Phoenix, I had a few other experiences that underscored for me the importance of always sticking to my moral compass. It is also important to decide whether to think on a short-term basis or a long-term basis. People who think on a short-term basis sometimes take shortcuts to get to their goals. Their moral compass is "tilted," and taking shortcuts won't bother them. Because we were operating a high-end clothing store and Phoenix is a winter tourist destination, some of our customers were imported gangsters who wanted to dress well, and they had the money to do so. It was my first introduction to them. Burned in my memory is the day one of those people phoned me and said, "Mort, I have a million dollars, and I need somebody to hold it for me. I'll pay you a lot of money to do that for me." Although a lot of money for a tiny effort clicked on a switch of immediate interest somewhere in the back of my mind, my moral compass was instantly on "high alert!" I knew that guy was shady, and I didn't want to be tainted by his kind of possibly illegal activity, nor assume the risk of doing something that could be illegal. I said "No, thank you—nice to talk to you, but no, thank you."

It was at this point that I began to discern the important difference between having a short-term view and a long-term view. I sure could have used the money that he was offering to me, and if I had operated from a short-term perspective, I might have accepted it—as many people would have done. I would have made (what was then) a lot of money in very little time. But my long-term perspective was that I didn't want my reputation to be sullied by engaging in a questionable business transaction with a crook. I didn't necessarily refuse to do the deal because I'm a "do-gooder"; I'm a capitalist, and a financier and a businessman, so I'm always looking for opportunities to increase my financial balance sheet. But no matter what the short-term benefit of that transaction might have been, there was a more important long-term problem associated with it: being tainted by the transaction, potential criminal liability, probably damaging my reputation, and the extreme likelihood that I would be pressured to get involved in future deceitful transactions, of which I wanted no part.

Benjamin Franklin has been credited with the saying, "He that lieth down with dogs shall rise up with fleas," meaning that you should be cautious of the company you keep. If you associate with people of bad reputation and bad character, that may not only damage your own reputation, it can also lead you astray because of the unscrupulous actions of those with low moral principles.

I had another opportunity to make money offered to me by a customer while I was in the retail business in Phoenix. He was another shady character and offered to send my wife and me to Las Vegas, making it clear that it was "on me and the boys." This was in the early days of Las Vegas where the word "boys" meant the mobster. The people in Las Vegas who were running a casino liked me, and they told me that if my wife and I moved to Las Vegas, they'd teach me the gambling business. Although making a solid connection like that had the potential to make me wealthy, this was during a time when if those people decided they didn't like you much, you could end up dead in the desert. Once again, my moral compass said, "I don't want to do this." So my response was, "No, thank you." I could have made a lot of money, but it violated my sense of right and wrong, and sense of self-preservation. A moral compass includes all of the above.

When you operate consistently with your moral compass in mind and refuse to take shortcuts, people will come to understand that you're trustworthy. If I owe you money, but don't have it to repay at this time, there are a couple of paths I can choose. The short-term path might be to default on our contract. Many people do that.

Wouldn't it be better for my long-term career, however, if instead I call you and say, "I don't have the money to pay you right now, but as soon as I have it, you're the first person I'll pay." You may not be happy that I can't pay you today, but the fact that I **will** pay you when I can makes me the exception to the rule. Will you stay with me? Will you continue to do business with me? Will others prefer to do business with me in the future? My experience is that 99 out of 100 people will respond, "Yes, thank you for calling me. Take care of it as soon as you can." I learned that by watching my dad's experiences with his retail store customers in Litchfield, Illinois: people want to do what's right, and we need to give them that opportunity when it's in our power.

Always acting in accordance with a long-term view can be painful at times, because people with a short-term view seem to make progress faster than those with a long-term view (unless you do something extremely rare, like invent the iPhone, or conversely, get caught breaking the law and go to prison). Most people have to "grind it out," step-by-step. You need to gather the knowledge, figure out where you're going to go, form a goal and make a plan. **You have to learn and have to figure out how to look for opportunity.** The more you learn, and the more you build your Mental Balance Sheet, the more you'll understand when you have experiences, whether or not there is an opportunity. If you don't know what you don't know, and you haven't broadened your thought process or knowledge base, opportunities will pass you by and you won't even realize it. The techniques I am describing should enable you to see and recognize opportunities when they arise.

Most people who survive over the long term in business are the people who have a strong moral compass based on high values. They know what they're willing to do, and what they're not willing to do. They operate within those parameters. They have good reputations, are trusted, and they don't deviate from their principles.

I had another opportunity to make a lot of money quickly when another somewhat shady person I'll call "Steve" approached me while I was operating the retail clothing store in Phoenix. Steve was a big guy, and mean as he could be—but he liked me, because I was personable, and I was a good salesman. One day Steve walked into the store and approached me, saying, "Listen Mort. We're going to rent a boat. We have a bunch of gold we 'picked up' down in Mexico. We're going to drive this gold up to the United States. Do you want to drive the boat?"

"Where are you going to be?" I asked.

He responded, "Me and a couple of other guys are going to be in the bottom of the boat with machine guns. If the Coast Guard comes, we'll take care of them."

I didn't have to consider his request for even a second. My immediate response was, "No."

Steve would have paid me big money to drive that boat—way more money than I was making in the clothing store. I liked driving boats, and if not for the gold, the United States Coast Guard, and the machine guns, I might have gone on the boat ride for free. Throwing a lot of money at me only made it better. But I was programmed NOT to do something like that. The immoral aspects and the danger were outside of my moral compass. If I had been a short-term thinker without the right moral base, I might have done it. Our prisons are full of people who thought the rewards greatly outweighed the risks involved. They were wrong, weren't they? There are lesser repercussions to choosing wrong than prison, but they will affect your long-term goals in life just as much. **It is important for you to have a moral compass and always stick by it.** Be of high character and surround yourself with people of high character: people who are motivated, intelligent, with goals similar to yours, and who do not take shortcuts to success. **Doing this will always serve you well, in life**

and in business. A strong moral compass is one of the most valuable assets on your Mental Balance Sheet. Associating with people of bad character is a liability on your Mental Balance Sheet.

CHAPTER FIVE – FORMING GOALS
Military Service (1958-1959)

While in college I became aware of the opportunities and training that a position in the military could provide me. Mandatory conscription or the draft into the military was the law of the United States at that time, and I decided that if I had to go into the Army, I wanted to enter the military as an officer—become an "officer and a gentleman," which would provide an opportunity to develop leadership skills, as well as provide other benefits, so I enrolled in the ROTC (Reserve Officers Training Corps) program as a freshman in college.   I attended ROTC basic training camp at Fort Riley, Kansas between my junior and senior years of college. It was a very tough experience—the Army intentionally roughed us up to see who could stay with it, and who would wash out. There were big sergeants hollering at me all the time, scaring me half to death. They'd give us nothing to drink for 24 hours, put us next to an M3 Howitzer 105 mm artillery cannon (while we were blindfolded, so we didn't know it was there) and pull a lanyard that would set off the cannon. The noise was deafening, and the experience was terrifying. The sergeants would stand nearby watching, to see what we'd do, and how we handled it. They also made us crawl through mud under machine gun fire and made us march for miles, all with nothing to drink. In today's world, I don't think the Army would treat people that way, unless they were in training for the Special Forces (like the Marines, Army Rangers or Navy Seals teams). I made it—didn't wash out. During ROTC, I trained in both infantry and artillery basics. In these days, all officers were first trained in infantry and I was also taught how to be an artillery Forward Observer.

A Forward Observer is the guy who climbs up on a hill, looks around, and decides when and where to call in artillery fire during a battle. By the way, this was not a good career position, because the average life expectancy in war-time of a deployed Forward Observer is about 24 hours, as enemy snipers try to pick them off as soon as possible. Subsequent to this, the Army gave me a Military Occupational Specialty (MOS): "artillery and guided missiles." I told my superiors that I was a philosophy student and a business student, and that I had studied economics and accounting and finance. I informed them that, "I'd be great in the Quartermaster Corp!" The job of a Quartermaster is to make sure equipment, materials and systems are available and functioning for missions. That sounded a lot more in line with my education than artillery and missiles did. But they insisted, "Lieutenant, you're going to artillery and missile school."

I received guided missile training at Fort Bliss, Texas, specifically on the Nike Ajax and Nike Hercules missiles, and I became a Launching Control Officer for guided missiles. Both the Nike Ajax and the Nike Hercules were surface-to-air missiles (SAM). Our government at the time was concerned that the Russians might attack us with bombers, so we were trained to fire those missiles at incoming enemy aircraft.

We were originally trained to operate the Nike Ajax, then later the Nike Hercules, which was an improved missile that used a plastic solid fuel and consequently wasn't as dangerous to fuel as the Nike Ajax was, which used red fuming nitric acid. When fueling the Nike Ajax missile, on both sides of us there were large mounds that looked like small Egyptian pyramids. We had to wear "spacesuits" to fuel the Ajax missiles all while staying within the pyramids. One drop of that fuel on your hand would go right through it! The missiles would rise up out of the ground, and we had to walk over to them with our spacesuits on and fuel them. Naturally, I was nervous all the time. It was a high-pressure, extremely volatile environment. Those missiles reached speeds of 2,000 mph very shortly after the "fire" button was pressed, and as the Launching Control Officer, I was responsible for when that button was going to be pressed.

Understanding how those guided missile systems worked provides a great analogy of **how to accomplish a goal**, which is a powerful asset for your Mental Balance Sheet. In the course of my guided missile training, it occurred to me that the human brain, properly programmed, will function similarly to the servo-mechanism in a missile. A servo-mechanism is defined as an automatic device used to correct the performance of a mechanism by means of an error-sensing feedback. The term servo-mechanism . . . properly applies only to systems in which the feedback and error-correction signals control mechanical position or one of its derivatives such as velocity or acceleration."[1] I know it sounds a little technical, so I'll break it down.

A rocket guidance system is made up of the following equipment:

a. Missile

b. Computer—Rocket Guidance System (RGS) (servo-mechanism)

c. Missile Track Radar (MTR)

d. Target Track Radar (TTR)

A number of steps occur, in the following sequence, during the launching of a guided missile:

1. A target is discovered, and the person manning the RGS computer terminal receives orders to destroy the target.

2. RGS sends information to the TTR, which begins its search for the target. TTR relays its findings back to the computer.

3. The missile is launched toward the target.

4. Missile Track Radar takes control and guides the missile to target.

Following is a graphic illustration of the foregoing steps:

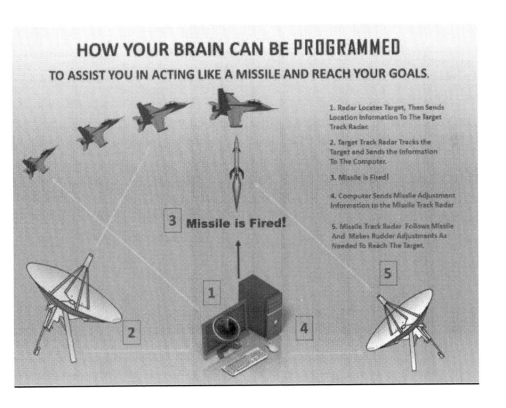

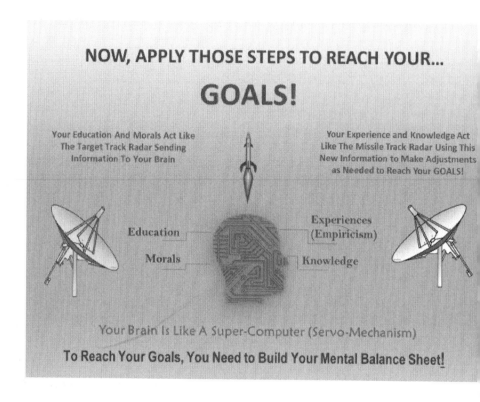

Later in life, and after reading *Psycho Cybernetics*, it became clear to me and I recognized the analogy that my brain was like the computer in the rocket guidance system. My goals were the target, and the knowledge, information, experiences, failures, successes and education acted like the target track radar in helping me to accomplish my goals.

In our practice scenario, an Air Force plane flew across the area pulling a target, and I would switch the button on the computer causing the radar to read it as 180 degrees out of phase, ensuring that we didn't accidentally blow anyone out of the sky. The missile would lock onto the target, and I would have someone watching the radar screen to tell me where the target was. Once fired, the target track radar (TTR) would send the target's position to the computer (RGS), which would, through the missile track radar (MTR), send the new position to the missile, causing the missile to change direction as necessary and to intercept and destroy the target.

One of my more memorable and educational (non-military) experiences while at Fort Bliss involved a trip to Mexico with some of the other officers. We decided to take a short drive down to the small town of Canutillo, not far from Parral, where Pancho Villa's ranch was.[2] Pancho Villa was a very colorful figure during the Mexican Revolution, a revolutionary and a leader of guerilla warfare, who fought against several Mexican dictators he believed were corrupt. He was a very violent man and had shot so many people that he greatly feared being shot himself. He never allowed anyone to walk behind him—not even in his own house.[3] On July 20, 1923, Pancho Villa was assassinated in an ambush in Parral, Chihuahua, Mexico. Seven or eight men were waiting for him, leaning rifles out the windows of a second-floor apartment, and when his car passed by, they opened fire. He was shot 9 times, dying instantly. More than 40 hollow-point bullets had hit his car. Most of the people who were with him also died. His widow still lived in Canutillo and still owned the car in which he was assassinated. We were lucky enough to meet her, and I asked Mrs. Villa, "How is it that he was so powerful?" She looked at me and answered, "Well, he had the gold, and he had the power—he was the boss." That brief reply really made an impact on my mind. Now I certainly don't agree with the way Pancho Villa *used* his power, but it does go to show that mental resources and financial assets like gold, in any pursuit, make the difference between success and failure. Lesson learned.

After completing my training at Fort Bliss, my first assignment was as a basic training company commander at Fort Leonard Wood, Missouri. Fort Leonard Wood was a pretty tough place. It's like the Parris Island (the Marine Corps recruit training facility) of the Army. I was in charge of a basic training company and had two big, really tough sergeants reporting to me. They knew all about basic training, while on the other hand, I was just learning about it. Although the two sergeants were under my command, they knew a lot more than I did about my job. The recruits entering basic training were 18 years old, and I was barely older at only 21, but I was in charge. I was beginning to gain some effective leadership skills, so I decided to draw from my Mental Balance Sheet, and I took these two sergeants aside and was very open with them: "Listen, as you know I'm recently commissioned and have a lot to learn," I told them. "You two know all about basic training. Will you help me learn?"

"Yes sir, Lieutenant!" they responded, and they were as good as their word. They looked out for me, and I looked out for them. Lesson learned: Use power carefully and wisely. Learn from and respect your subordinates and you and they will perform well. "**HELP ME**" is one of the most powerful request motivators in our culture. I have used it often and effectively throughout my business career and personal life.

When the recruits were undergoing basic training, we initially conducted what we called a "mass destruction," to show them what the military could accomplish with a little of its special brand of firepower. First, the Air Force would open fire with airplanes overhead, strafing the area, then the artillery would start firing 50 caliber machine guns on the back of half-tracks, along with 75 or 90 mm cannons and flamethrowers. The new recruits were observing and glad they were in a safe place. Nothing could have lived, nothing breathed—there was total devastation out there in the middle of the demonstration area. This was the kind of experience we put the young recruits through, to help them understand what it would be like in a real war situation. As in many circumstances, the teacher learned more than the students did. I learned a lot from putting the young recruits through their basic training, but it didn't take long for me to figure out that the military wasn't my favorite experience and I certainly didn't want to make it my career.

Another interesting experience that I remember while fulfilling my responsibilities as the Basic Training Company Commander is as follows: one of the new recruits going through basic training was a young Jewish kid from Chicago, something I knew about. He was kind of a "momma's boy," and he never seemed to get anything right. When the men were marching, the sergeants would call out the cadence of "Left, right! Left, right!" But this guy was never on the correct foot. I don't know if he just didn't know his left from his right, or what the problem was, but he was always mixed up and had difficulties performing most tasks. Finally, one day I realized that I needed to "recycle" him, which meant that he would have to start basic training all over again. He just wasn't learning what he needed to know. Shortly after I made the decision to recycle the recruit, I received a call that the Colonel wanted to see me. I was a little nervous going to his office, and after I walked in and introduced myself, the Colonel told me: "Lieutenant Fleischer, we have received a complaint that you are an anti-Semite!"

I could hardly keep from smiling as I retorted, "Colonel, I have to tell you, that's a little hard to believe. I may not be formally religious, but I am Jewish myself. The recruit didn't know what he was doing and I did my job by recycling him, hoping to help him."

The Colonel smiled and said, "You know, we're glad to have you Lieutenant. We need more officers like you. You're excused." Lesson Learned: when you believe you are right, take action accordingly!

My experiences as the Basic Training Company Commander provided some valuable assets for my Mental Balance Sheet: as I (1) began to grasp basic leadership principles; (2) developed an understanding of the value of respect, courage, character, and the power of individual motivation; (3) learned the necessity for, and how to develop teamwork; and (4) I discovered the valuable principle of giving people responsibility and then holding them accountable to execute that responsibility. This is the principle we began discussing at the beginning of the chapter, because giving people responsibility and holding them accountable to execute it is a great "sorter" of people. In the Army, if you didn't execute your responsibilities, you washed out. In the business world, if you don't execute your responsibilities, you wash out, too.

Your Mind is a Sophisticated Computer, Your Personal Servo-mechanism

As we discussed earlier, when I began reading *Psycho-Cybernetics*, it became clear to me that there were many important concepts in the book, and it had a major impact on my thinking. "Psycho" means "Soul," or "Self," while "Cybernetics" has to do with technology: the goal-striving, goal-oriented behavior of mechanical systems—an internal system of self-correction that keeps you on a chosen course. I learned that the brain and nervous system constitute a complex goal-striving mechanism, which can act, depending on how you use it, as a built-in automatic guidance system for **achieving goals** that you set for it. I compared this information to what I had learned about _**missile guidance systems**_ in the military. It became clear that if I added my knowledge of the philosophic school of _**empiricism**_ (we are a sum of all our experiences) to the other important tools (intellectual capital) that I had now acquired, my _**servo-mechanism**_ (self-guiding and correcting brain) and experiences (empiricism), could lead me to my goal. In retrospect I look at these three tools as legs on my "three-legged" stool for success in business and life.

The information, experiences, failures, successes and education you experience are processed by your brain, which is analogous to the computer in the Rocket Guidance System. Your brain servo-mechanism (which is the best "computer" known to man) then **formulates goals** based on the information, experiences, failures, successes and education you have acquired, and you "launch" a decision to achieve those goals, much as the computer in the Rocket Guidance System launches the missile toward the target. As stated in _Psycho-Cybernetics_, "You do not need to be an electrical engineer or a physicist to operate your own servo-mechanism, any more than you need to engineer an automobile in order to drive one, or become an electrical engineer in order to turn on a light."[4] After you formulate a goal, if you really want to achieve it and begin to think intensely about the variables involved in achieving that goal, your "creative mechanism" will go to work, your servo-mechanism (brain) will scan back through the knowledge stored in it and will find an answer to achieve that goal. As stated in _Psycho-Cybernetics_, your mind:

". . . selects an idea here, a fact there, a series of former experiences, and relates them – or 'ties them together' into a meaningful whole which will 'fill out' the incomplete portion of your situation, complete your equation or 'solve' your problem. When this solution is served up to your consciousness – often at an unguarded moment when you are thinking of something else – or perhaps even as a dream while your consciousness is asleep – something 'clicks' and you at once 'recognize' this as the answer you have been searching for."[5]

Take the time now to continue completing the blank Mental Balance Sheet, filling in the assets you think I gained and liabilities I acquired based on what you have read thus far about my life and military experiences.

Compare the assets and liabilities you wrote in my Mental Balance Sheet with the assets and liabilities I noted myself for my Mental Balance Sheet after my experiences in the military. As you can see from the following representation, I gained some valuable assets from my military experience. In addition, as I mentioned previously, my college education and military service helped me to overcome some of my weaknesses, and you may notice that some of my former liabilities no longer appear on my Mental Balance Sheet:

ADDITIONS TO MR. FLEISCHER'S
MENTAL BALANCE SHEET
1958-1959 (Military Service)

ASSETS	LIABILITIES
Empirical Knowledge:	I *still* didn't know what I didn't know

- Basic leadership principles
- The need to develop and encourage teamwork
- Give people responsibility and make them responsible

Intellectual Capital:

- The operation of a missile guidance system and how it works
- How to use your brain as a goal seeking guidance system (servo-mechanism)

Moral Compass:

- Acquired a deeper understanding the value of respect courage, character and individual motivation

CHAPTER NOTES

[1] *Encyclopaedia Britannica.* "Servo-mechanism." www.britannica.com. Accessed December 15, 2015.
[2] Katz, Freiderich. *The Life and Times of Pancho Villa.* Stanford University Press, 1998. Cited in "Pancho Villa: The Assassination," www.laits.utexas.edu. Accessed January 20, 2016.
[3] *Ibid.*
[4]*Psycho-Cybernetics*, p.28.
[5]*Ibid.*, p.26.

CHAPTER SIX – ACHIEVING YOUR GOALS

Retail Business (1960-1962)

After completing my military service in the Army from 1958 to 1959, I started my first business enterprise: an upscale retail men's clothing store in Phoenix, Arizona, which I've already briefly discussed. I formed a partnership with my cousin's husband, who was about 20 years older than I was, and had acted much like a parent in helping me after my parents passed away. He was a truly good guy. I'd had some prior experience in retailing, working for the Stix, Baer, Fuller and May Department Stores in St. Louis while I was in college. Our Phoenix store carried very high-end merchandise, like alligator shoes, mohair suits, and other expensive clothing. A lot of "wanna-be" flaky men came into the store, but they couldn't really afford the clothing. Many of the successful people of Phoenix shopped in our store—as did the gangsters I've told you about. They walked in with a lot of money, and they liked to wear expensive clothing. I could almost always predict when a restaurant in Phoenix was going to burn down, because thugs from Chicago and/or New York would come into the store, and buy alligator shoes, fancy Italian pants and suits. Like clockwork, there was often a fire shortly after a big sale to a fancy dresser from out of town!

Although I did pretty well operating a clothing store, I didn't particularly like the retail business, and found it to be very confining. However, I did gain some very helpful assets for my Mental Balance Sheet, as I learned about marketing, operating and financing a small business. I also gained helpful empirical knowledge as I learned about human nature and the fundamentals of measuring and filling consumer desires, which could sometimes be somewhat irrational. For example, occasionally a customer with a huge stomach would enter the store after eyeing a particular suit in the front window, and wanted me to help him try on that suit. They usually expected me to make them look like movie stars! I got them as close as possible, although they often didn't give me much to work with. One thing I learned is that people always wanted the suit in the window. It always looked great on the mannequin, mainly because we pinned it into place to look great, no matter how it was actually cut. I learned that if I wanted to get rid of a particular suit, I displayed it in the front window of the store, and it would sell. I gained knowledge regarding how humans react to different images and stimuli—which is what a salesman and businessman should learn to become successful.

Although I actually felt a little restricted by the retail business, during that time I gained some vital knowledge relevant to how to achieve my goals when I read a recently published book titled *Psycho-Cybernetics*, by Dr. Maxwell Maltz (published by Simon & Schuster in 1960.) *Psycho-Cybernetics* contains a chapter titled "Discovering Your

Success Mechanism," which I found fascinating and very helpful as I made plans to leave retailing and engage in a business pursuit that would be more satisfying to me. At that point my goal for my life's work had begun to take form: I began to understand that I wanted to build a company (or companies) that added value to my investors, customers, myself and the system. I didn't know exactly what kind of company I wanted to build, but it became my goal and I constantly **kept that goal in mind** as I engaged in the various business ventures of my career. I felt that building a company to my own design would be an exciting and fulfilling life's journey.

Unfortunately, this was contrary to what the remnants of my family thought—they felt I should become a doctor, lawyer, or Certified Public Accountant (CPA). However, I was beginning to realize that I was an entrepreneur (although I could hardly spell the word). There weren't very many entrepreneurs in the 1960s, certainly not like there are now. The growing assets of my Mental Balance Sheet had become substantial enough to be helpful to me. I realized that I needed more of those assets to enable me to reach my goal of creating a business of substance that would meet my goals. I wasn't sure what kind of a business it would be, but I knew based on my philosophical studies that I needed to have experiences. I needed to pursue what came close to me, and what looked interesting to me, that fit my moral compass, business goals, vision and strategy. I was consciously studying and utilizing Dr. Maltz' principles of success outlined in *Psycho-Cybernetics*, which hold that we all are "engineered for success and happiness." The book sets forth five basic principles by which our success mechanisms operate. Because these principles are still foundational to personal success, let's consider them together:

(1) Your built-in success mechanism must have a goal or "target." This goal, or target must be conceived of as "already in existence—now," either in actual or potential form. It operates by either (a) steering you to a goal already in existence, or by (b) "discovering" something already in existence.

(2) The automatic mechanism is teleological. That is, it operates or must be oriented to "end results" or goals. Do not be discouraged because the "means whereby" may not be apparent. It is the function of the automatic mechanism to supply the goal. Think in terms of the end result, and the means whereby it will be achieved will often take care of themselves.

(3) Do not be afraid of making mistakes, or of temporary failures. All servo-mechanisms achieve a goal by recognizing negative feedback, or by going forward, making mistakes, and immediately correcting course.

(4) Skill learning of any kind is accomplished by trial and error, mentally correcting aim after an error, until a

successful motion, movement, or performance has been achieved. *After that*, further learning and continued success, is accomplished by *forgetting the past errors, and remembering the successful response*, so that it can be "imitated."

(5) You must learn to trust your creative mechanism to do its work and not just "jam it" by becoming too concerned or too anxious as to whether or not it will work, or by attempting to force it through too much conscious effort. You must "let" it work, rather than "make" it work. This trust is necessary because your creative mechanism operates below your level of consciousness, and you cannot "know" what is going on beneath the surface. Moreover, its nature is to operate *spontaneously* according to *present need*. Therefore, you have no guarantees in advance. It comes into operation *as you act* and as you place demand upon it by your actions. You must not wait to act until you have proof—you must act as if it is there, and it will come through.

Dr. Maltz recommended memorizing those five basic principles, and I believe you, the student, will greatly benefit from doing so. They will help you in **forming your goals** for your life. Being familiar with these principles will also cast "additional light" on the rest of the principles discussed in this book.

"Do the thing and you will have the power," said

Emerson.[1]

As I mentioned, my goal was to design a business that would provide an exciting and fulfilling long-term life's journey. It is my hope that the Fleischer Scholars Program will be a first step in your journey of creating a goal for the business career you will eventually pursue.

America affords almost limitless opportunities for careers in business and for creating new businesses. There are many types of business careers, such as entrepreneurs, intrapreneurs (a person employed by a large organization that creates a new venture), professional managers, stockbrokers, and hedge fund managers, to name just a few. The following list of industries is a small sampling of very general categories of the almost unlimited business pursuits that are available in the United States:

Agriculture, Forestry, Fishing and Hunting
Mining
Utilities (Gas, Electricity, Communications)
Construction
Manufacturing
Transportation and Warehousing

Information
Wholesale Trade
Retail Trade
Finance, Commercial Banking, Investment Banking, Insurance
Real Estate Development, Finance, Rental, and Leasing
Professional, Scientific and Technical Services
Management of Companies and Enterprises
Administrative and Support and Waste Management and
Remediation Services
Education Services
Health Care and Social Assistance
Arts, Entertainment and Recreation
Accommodation and Food Services
Public Administration

Within each of the foregoing categories many career opportunities exist. For example, in the world of banking, careers are available in community banking, regional banking, and investment banking. Possibilities in manufacturing are limited only by your imagination. Companies exist in every size. There are different business organizational structures (*e.g.*, partnerships, corporations, and limited liability companies), and they may be privately or publicly owned. You can choose to pursue any kind of business endeavor, whether it's owning a gas station or building the next Tesla Motor Company. A student in the Fleischer Scholars Program years ago told me that he "wanted to build a company like General Electric." My response was, "then you'd better not sit here too long!"

Another student in the Fleischer Scholars Program once commented to me, "Mr. Fleischer, you have had a lot of jobs!" I responded by saying that the various business enterprises in which I'd engaged during my career were not jobs, but rather learning experiences from which I'd **gained assets** for my **Mental Balance Sheet**, and they helped me to **accomplish my ultimate goal of building a business of substance to my design**. From each of those business opportunities I acquired knowledge, experience and skills that added assets to my Mental Balance Sheet. And no matter what I was doing at the time, I always kept my ultimate goal in mind. As I continued to acquire knowledge through my various business enterprises, my ultimate goal gradually became better defined. For example, after two years handling mergers and acquisitions (1968-1970), it became apparent to me that finding companies and/or a niche that needed financing and capital that the system wasn't providing, was where the opportunity I was seeking existed.

Stay Focused on Your Goal

One of my management techniques that I began to learn in the military and refined over time is designed to find out which employee can actually be effective at accomplishing goals. That technique is to "give people responsibility and make them responsible." Interestingly enough, when most people hear this principle, they respond by saying that they believe they would like to operate in this manner and think that they can do so creatively, effectively and efficiently. My experience has been decidedly mixed. Most people can be responsible on a small scale. However, as the obligations and goals become more complex and are on a larger scale, the number of people that have the motivation and can operate at this level becomes decidedly smaller.

I noticed this low percentage of people and decided I needed to develop an illustration for goal achievement that might increase the number of people who could more effectively set and accomplish goals without getting **bogged down by distractions**. This is illustrated by the story of the Man, the Mouse and the Cheese which follows:

If you put a piece of cheese wedge in the corner of a room and you have a human on one side of the room and a mouse on the other side, who is going to get the cheese first? The human is likely to say, "Why is that cheese out of place and in that corner? Who put it there? Is it clean sitting on the floor? It might be rotten . . . and so on. The mouse says, "WOW! That looks like a great cheese wedge!" and goes directly to get it. The mouse always gets the cheese.

The mouse didn't worry about every detail or that the cheese didn't quite fit his model of expectation, or that he might have to get out of his comfort zone and run across the room to beat the human to it. Out of fear of failure or concerns that they might be wrong, humans have developed a number of bad habits, causing them to hesitate, over-evaluate, and generally resist change, rather than deciding promptly, being highly motivated, and trusting their own judgment.

To me the symptoms of being easily distracted from one's goal are illustrative of an improperly programmed mind-servo-mechanism.

I suggest to people that practicing the techniques I learned from *Psycho-Cybernetics* have helped me immensely, and I have noticed substantial improvement in others that have done the same. We are awash in information, detail and the ever-present human desire to be secure and comfortable in the goals we set and decisions we make. You have to learn how to sort, and to eliminate the distractions. My view of life is that I can't learn everything; I want to learn how to use what is around me to accomplish my goals and get to where I'd like to be in life.

Clearing your mind of the tendency to be distracted by minutiae, and programming it to simultaneously and effectively set and attain goals will allow you to develop better instincts. As I mentioned previously, I define instincts as the working of your subconscious mind which will assist you in achieving your goals. In short, you will develop judgment and, with hard work and time, wisdom. Many people lack the crucial Mental Balance Sheet assets of judgment and wisdom.

Take this opportunity to complete the blank Mental Balance Sheet you've been filling in for me, filling in the assets I gained and liabilities I acquired based on what you have read thus far about my life and experiences in the retail business.

Now compare the assets and liabilities you wrote in the blank Mental Balance Sheet with the assets and liabilities I noted myself for my Mental Balance Sheet after my experiences in the retail business.

ADDITIONS TO MR. FLEISCHER'S
MENTAL BALANCE SHEET
1960-1962 (Retail Business)

ASSETS	LIABILITIES
Empirical Knowledge:	I *still* didn't know what I didn't know

Empirical Knowledge:

- Learned customer service
- Learned that I needed to focus on my goals and not get bogged down with the minutiae
- Value of and how to use marketing and advertising
- How to achieve goals
- Discovered my success mechanism and how it operates (*Psycho Cybernetics*)

Intellectual Capital:

- Marketing
- Advertising
- Small business operations

Moral Compass:

- Stay true to the courage of my convictions And stay true to my value system

CHAPTER NOTES

[1]Maltz, Dr. Maxwell. *Psycho-Cybernetics.* Simon & Schuster, New York. 1960. p. 29.

CHAPTER SEVEN – LIFE INSURANCE SALES AND THE ART OF COMMUNICATION (1963-1967)

The retail men's clothing store that I operated in Phoenix with my cousin, as I've mentioned, carried very stylish, expensive clothing. Consequently, most of the customers were "men of means." I noticed that some customers who were in the life insurance business were able to buy a lot of high-priced clothing. As we became acquainted, I asked them how they conducted business, and they explained it to me as follows.

At this time (the early to mid-1960s), there were quite a few new life insurance companies being formed that were selling "founders" policies (which amounted to "getting in on the ground floor" of the companies). The life insurance companies were formed with the minimum capitalization required by the state in which they operated, and they began to market life insurance to a limited number of "founders." Typically, they would require as a minimum, for example, a $5,000 annual premium. They would then show the prospect how much money the large, well-known, well-capitalized insurance companies, such as New York Life made, and contractually commit that the first 10,000 founders would be entitled to 1/3 of the profits of the new company. Using New York Life as an example, assuming the new company could grow to be equally as large, 1/3 of the profits divided by 10,000 equaled a substantial amount of money, which the owner of the policy would receive each year in the form of dividends.

In this scenario, the prospect's child became the insured, which would result in a lower risk to the insurance company (due to the greater longevity of the child), and the sales prospect would be the policy owner and receive the dividends. Upon the prospect's demise, ownership of the policy would revert to the child. To simplify: the life insurance salesmen were selling profit-sharing ordinary life insurance, which was low risk to the insurer, because the insureds were children with long actuarial longevity. The risks were reinsured with a large, well-capitalized insurance company. Consequently, many of the new life insurance companies were approved by the various states' Insurance Commissioners, because their risks were actuarially sound. Commissions to the salespeople were high, hence their ability to shop in our men's store and buy expensive clothing.

Chafing at the restrictiveness of retailing clothing, and **keeping in mind my goal** to create a more interesting business at some point in the future, I decided to get out of the retail business, and sold my interest to my partner. I subsequently went to work selling "founders" policies for a new life insurance company. I decided that prospects would be better in the Midwest, so I moved our family from Phoenix to St. Louis, Missouri.

I was doing well financially selling founders policies for the new life insurance company when a relative of mine noticed an ad in the newspaper about another new life insurance company that was for sale in Lafayette, Louisiana. The company was having financial difficulties. Lafayette was my Mother-in-law's hometown. I travelled to Lafayette, and contracted for an option to purchase the company for $500,000 by putting down $5,000, which was half of all the cash that I had at this time.

Shortly thereafter, a gentleman from Connecticut General Life Insurance Company, a big life insurance company that reinsured the new life insurance companies, introduced me to Charlie Sharpe. Charlie was the founder and successful operator of another relatively new life insurance company named "Ozark National Life." In return for my conveying to him my option to purchase the financially troubled company, Charlie agreed to recapitalize my optioned company, go to the Louisiana Insurance Commissioner and get the company re-licensed, and then bring in new operational and sales personnel. I recognized that Charlie Sharpe had access to capital and the knowledge and experience that I was lacking. Seeing it as a good opportunity, I traded him my option in return for 20% ownership of the new company. It was a good trade.

We quickly moved to Lafayette, Louisiana where I became a Senior Vice-President of the new company and proceeded to sell founders' policies and help build the new company.

Charlie Sharpe was very successful. He sold a lot of insurance, and I learned many valuable skills from him. Charlie taught me how to be a good direct salesman (where the prospect is contacted personally), and many of the important points of what I now call "the art of communication." Communication is an extremely valuable business skill. It's an important art that I believe the world is losing because of all of our electronic devices. Those devices eliminate face-to-face communication, which is crucial in life, and especially in the business world.

One of my more memorable (and educational) experiences working with Charlie was when the two of us went to see the Louisiana Insurance Commissioner to get the license renewed for the new insurance company we were going to recapitalize. We were in a room on about the 20th floor of the Huey Long Building (the Louisiana State Capitol in Baton Rouge is 34 stories tall and the tallest capitol building in the United States), meeting with the Assistant Insurance Commissioner and a couple of other men who worked for the Louisiana Department of Insurance. The Assistant Insurance Commissioner looked at Charlie and announced, "Mr. Sharpe, we've checked you out, and we're not sure we agree with some of your earlier sales practices. And we don't think you're telling us the whole truth."

Charlie's blood pressure skyrocketed so fast, it was almost visible as he leaped out of his chair! Charlie was a big mid-western farmer and a strong man. He grabbed the Assistant Insurance

Commissioner, and in his Midwestern Missouri accent shouted, "No man alahv calls me a liar! I'm going to throw you out the winder!" Charlie grabbed the man, dragged him over to the window of the high rise, and threatened to throw him out of the window! Fortunately, the Insurance Commissioner walked in just then and intervened, exclaiming, "Hold on, Mr. Sharpe! That's not the way we do things in Louisiana!"

Charlie immediately released the man. Unfortunately, the Insurance Commissioner then continued, "We don't hear good things about what you do." Apparently Charlie's blood pressure had not yet returned to normal, because he looked at him and retorted venomously,

> "Let me tell you something, Sir! I know a lot about how you operate here! And I want this license, and we run a clean operation. And I know a lot about you guys. And if Mort and I don't get this license by Monday morning, I'm going straight to the *Times-Picayune* newspaper in New Orleans and telling them everything I know about you! Come on, Mort!"

he yelled it as he stormed out of the room. So we left, and I hurried after him, considerably unnerved. My wife was 8 months pregnant, I only had $5,000 left in the bank, and I had left a good job in St. Louis. I couldn't imagine we were going to receive the license we needed to operate the new company, and I was pretty depressed about this turn of events. But the following Monday morning we did receive that insurance license! Charlie's bluff had worked! Apparently, the insurance commission men had lived their lives in such a way that a bluff to reveal their gray activities and questionable character was sufficient to get a license from them. From that experience I learned more valuable skills—assets for my Mental Balance Sheet, including:

(1) More about the art of bluffing;

(2) More about the art of negotiation;

(3) The fact that it is crucial to know your opponent; and

(4) Always to be prepared.

Not everyone you deal with in the business world will have the same value system you do, and it's important to know how to deal with those people. Charlie Sharpe knew exactly with whom he was dealing and the right way to negotiate with them. As a result, he got what he wanted: our license to sell life insurance and to run a life insurance company in Louisiana.

I learned another valuable business practice while working in Louisiana: it is crucial to know the environment in which you are operating. My Mother-in-law was from an old Louisiana family in Lafayette. Trying to help "jump-start" my career in Louisiana, she phoned the Governor, John McKeithen, and told him, "I'd like you to meet my son-in-law." I was young, in my mid-20s, and was a little bit intimidated to be meeting the Governor. But I went to meet him, and as he shook my hand he looked me in the eye and announced, "You come from a nice family. Mr. Fleischer, we're glad to have you here, and your family has been in Louisiana a long time. If there's anything I can do for you that's of a legal nature, you let me know!" After thinking about it for a second, he added, "You know what? Even if it isn't legal, you let me know!" And with that, he made me a colonel on the Governor's staff, giving me a card and a little badge.

There was power in that little card! I would speed around Louisiana, sometimes even running red lights while I called on people to sell life insurance. When the State Patrol would stop me I'd show that little card as I pulled out my driver's license, and the officer would say, "Just slow down, will you, please, Mr. Fleischer?!"

The Governor and his staff ran the state. That was another important lesson I learned while selling life insurance there: in order to get to know the environment you are in, answer for yourself the questions, "how does this place work?" and "how do the people here think?" Most of all, it's crucial to know how you are going to deal with in an environment and yet, within your moral framework, get where you want to be.

I learned another valuable lesson while working with Charlie Sharpe on the new insurance company. In order to capitalize the company, we needed to raise $700,000. Charlie was able to raise that money, and I'll always remember the day he returned to Louisiana and walked into our company boardroom with all that money stuffed in his pocket. It was all in the form of checks and cash, and Charlie reached into his pocket and dumped it all on the board table, announcing, "Here's the money, Mort—let's go close this thing!" But he had forgotten to file a registration statement with the Securities and Exchange Commission (S.E.C.), and because of that omission, we had technically violated the Securities Act of 1933, a very important Federal law with possible criminal penalties for failure to comply. Charlie had raised the funds without the proper S.E.C. clearance! I had to hire lawyers in Dallas, who told me that we had to give the investors a "rescission offer," which offered them their money back if they weren't happy at that point. We filed the registration statement, and thankfully, none of the investors wanted their money back, because the stock was trading at a higher price than when they had initially invested. We were very fortunate—if the investors had wanted their money back, the company would have failed. It was a valuable lesson to me, to always be sure my business enterprises complied with all applicable laws and regulations and to hire competent lawyers when complicated projects begin.

Charlie Sharpe was the greatest salesman I've ever seen. In his monthly sales meetings Charlie would speak in front of 500 people and absolutely enthrall them. He'd completely captivate his audience talking about the big insurance companies, how they had so much money, and how we were going to "do the right thing for our people." Charlie was so gifted at motivating people in sales meetings; it was almost like a religious experience. The sales force sold many policies and the company thrived.

My experiences observing and working with Charlie Sharpe provided some very significant assets for my Mental Balance Sheet. I learned:

   a.   How life insurance companies operate and are financed;

   b.   How actuaries work—about statistics and probability;

c. How insurance companies can earn money on their liabilities;

d. How to turn an option on a company (small investment) into a substantial profit by making a bargain purchase and converting my option into a substantial position in a recapitalized company;

e. The importance of operating a business within the parameters of the law, and to always comply with applicable laws and regulations (okay, except for speed limits);

f. The importance of knowing the environment in which you're operating; and

g. *Most importantly*, Charlie taught me the art of becoming a direct salesman and master communicator, which would provide the foundation for what I now call, and refined over time, the "Art of Communication." It is a critical skill to running any business enterprise, but it is especially crucial when running a business that is in the world of sales. From observing the way Charlie did things, I also learned the basics of the critical communication arts of bluffing and of negotiation.

Life Insurance-Direct Sales

As I continued to work in the life insurance industry and engaged in the direct sales of insurance policies, I learned more about the Art of Communication. Recently, in a quarterly meeting of S|T|O|R|E Capital (the company that I am currently Chairman of), I threw an old Blackberry phone on the floor and jumped up and down on it. The point that I graphically illustrated is that through the use of technology, people are losing the ability to communicate with one another. Looking another person in the eye and discussing face-to-face what you collectively would like to accomplish will have a much more positive result than sending an email. The following somewhat prophetic statement has been attributed to Albert Einstein:

> "I fear the day that technology will surpass our human interaction. The world will have a generation of idiots."

Certain strategies are crucial to learning the art of communication, including (1) the benefits of practicing your sales presentation, (2) communicating by asking questions, (3) knowing when to stop talking and listen to the prospect, (4) the power of third-party referrals, and (5) how to qualify a sales prospect.

A. Practice your sales presentation. In my opinion, many people appear to be afraid of having a face-to-face discussion, and in some instances, they are afraid of confrontation. I believe that clear, concise, personal communication is one of the major keys to being successful.

In your future business endeavors, before you present your   product to a potential investor or customer, or an idea or suggestion to a colleague, make sure you know all the details of that product or idea—inside and out. All good sales presentations are memorized. Practice selling the concept of the benefits of your product, goal or idea until you can start at the middle, beginning or end and can say it with enthusiasm and confidence. Practice in front of a mirror! This will help build your confidence. Remember, your brain and nervous system can't tell the difference between whether you are practicing or are in an actual presentation. Consequently, you will be programmed, more polished and have more confidence when making a real presentation. Once I learned this principle, I'd memorize my entire presentation, so that I could start anywhere in it.

Dr. Maxwell Maltz explained this principle in *Psycho-Cybernetics* when he quoted Charles B. Roth's book *How to Make $25,000 a Year Selling*[1] ($25,000 was a lot of money when the book was published). Roth told about a group of salesmen in Detroit who had increased their sales by 100% when they tried a new idea. Individual salesmen using the same idea increased their sales by up to 400%:

And what is this magic that accomplishes so much for salesmen?

It is something called role-playing, and you should know about it, because if you will let it, it may help you to double your sales.

What is role-playing?

Well, it is simply *imagining* yourself in various sales situations, then solving them *in your mind*, until you know what to say and what to do whenever the situation comes up in real life.

It is what is called on the football field "skull practice."

The reason why it accomplishes so much is that selling is simply a matter of situations.

One is created every time you talk to a customer. He says something or asks a question or raises an objection. If you always know how to counter what he says or answer his question or handle the objection, you make sales...

A role-playing salesman, at night when he is alone, will create these situations. He will imagine the prospect throwing the widest kind of curves at him. Then he will work out the best answer to them...

No matter what the situation is, you can prepare for it beforehand by means of imagining yourself and your prospect face to face while he is raising objections and creating problems and you are handling them properly.[2]

As also pointed out by Dr. Maltz, even if none of the situations you rehearsed come up, the rehearsal practice will still work wonders, because it will increase your confidence.

B. Communication through asking questions. I have enhanced the qualifying technique that I learned in selling insurance into a much subtler technique for communicating with my business associates and others in everyday life. I communicate by providing clear information, and establishing an achievable goal, and then asking a closing question of the other party such as, "Do you think this suggestion will work?" or, "I have a new idea, may I explain it?" When the other person agrees, I explain my new idea, and then ask, "What do you think of the idea?" **Always ask a closing question** after explaining an idea or making a point. You can't reach a goal until you know if the other party understands what you have said, what they are thinking or what comments or objections they may have. To reiterate, once you ask a closing question, **be quiet and wait for an answer**, no matter how long it takes for the other person to respond. If they agree with you, then go forward. If they have objections or suggestions, discuss them and clarify to be sure you understand their points, then move forward towards your goal. I call this technique "communication through asking questions." I try not to ask a question if I don't already know the answer to it. This technique allows me to see what the other party understands, and what the other party agrees or disagrees with regarding our discussion. Remember, you cannot convince someone unless you know what they are thinking. Asking questions is the key.

As you refine this technique, you will begin to have a better understanding of how people assimilate and process information, and subsequently make a decision. Remember, decisions are difficult for some people to make and it is human nature to resist change. A pattern will develop and you will get very good at knowing what the other person is thinking and how they will respond. Perfecting this communication technique will be **invaluable to you in your daily endeavors toward achieving your goals.**

C. Third-Party Referrals. A third-party referral is the greatest sales introduction and communication technique in the world. I received my first introduction to the power of a third-party referral during the years when I was traveling around the countryside, making direct sales of life insurance to Louisiana farmers. I would take note of the name of a prospective customer on their mailbox, then knock on their door. When the homeowner answered the door, I would introduce myself by saying, "Hello, Mr. _____ (name on the mailbox), I'm Mort Fleischer. Do you know Karen Johnson? (name from a neighbor's mailbox.) Do you like her? She sent me over here." So almost immediately I got myself into the house. Once I got into the house, the next step was to qualify the prospect.

D. Qualifying the Prospect. It is important to bring up the major decision-making objections at the beginning of your meeting, even before you explain why you are there. Don't be afraid to "take it away from them" under the theory that people want what they can't have. If you tell the prospect that "It isn't everyone that can qualify for this opportunity and we have a limited amount available." Then their interest level is generally peaked. There are certain sets of circumstances people use to make decisions. You need to help them make a decision. When you are making a sales presentation, both the husband and the wife need to be present. That helps avoid the situation where, at the end of the presentation, the husband says, "I need to ask my wife." When making direct sales, I always insisted that both the husband and the wife were present to hear it.

1. When selling a product to a married couple, playing on the female instincts of the wife is also a helpful strategy. I usually asked the wife if she would please bring me a glass of water. I knew that she would "like me better" if she had done something for me. By getting me a glass of water, the wife had an opportunity to help me, and she would have a subliminal positive reaction to that.

2. A good strategy is to ask the couple, "Do you two make your own decisions? If I show you something really attractive this evening, will you be able to make a decision now? Will you be able to tell me either 'yes' or 'no' at the end of my presentation?" This strategy helps eliminate another potential roadblock at the end of a presentation. Make sure in advance that your prospect is able to make a decision/commitment in a timely manner.

3. Clarify that the prospect has funds available for the investment. Ask the prospect whether, if you present him an exceptional opportunity, he would be able to invest $100,000. Continue to ask and reduce the amount of investment until he says "yes" to an

amount that you like. This strategy avoids the situation where the prospect tells you, "I don't have any money to invest" after you have put in the effort to make a presentation.

4. Ask the prospects for their "help" in building the company. "HELP" is one of the most powerful words in our culture. I continually ask people to help me, and very frequently receive a positive response. People like to feel that they've helped someone, and they become invested in you and your success if they've given you their help. Culturally, I have come to believe that asking for "HELP" (as I have previously mentioned) is the most powerful motivator in our society.

As you wind up your presentation, remind the prospect that, "Not everyone can qualify for this because we only have a limited amount." Take advantage of human nature, that people "want what they can't have." Take it away and close.

To summarize:

a.   Know your subject matter.

b.   Ask closing questions. You can't sell or communicate if you don't know what the other party's mindset is. When you ask a closing question, be quiet, listen, and wait for an answer. No matter how long it takes. (If it helps you to stay quiet, think to yourself, "The next person who talks loses!")

c.   Ignore minutia. It will upset your goal-seeking mechanism. *Stay focused!*

d. Exhibit excitement and enthusiasm! It is contagious and motivates people to act.

e. You can modify these qualifying techniques to most situations where decisions are required in your daily activities.

f. Don't hide from issues you believe the other party may object to. Bring them up initially and eliminate them in the manner the foregoing technique illustrates.

Over time I began to be more aware of just how big the large life insurance companies were and, though possible, I thought it would be difficult and would take years to build the Ozark National Companies. I sincerely wanted to build a large insurance company, but I realized it would be very difficult due to the large balance sheets that big life insurance companies have. They are difficult to replicate, which creates a ceiling in the life insurance world for new companies. Most of all, I wanted to continue pursuing my personal goal of building a company of my own design, although the vehicle and method of what I wanted to build wasn't yet clear to me.

I consequently decided to offer my 20% ownership interest in the life insurance company to Mr. Sharpe, and he agreed to buy my shares from me. At that time, my wife and I had two children. We decided to move our family back to Phoenix from Louisiana. I had gained a tremendous amount of empirical (personal experiences), knowledge, working with and observing Charlie Sharpe, and learning the art of communication, but I felt it was time to return to my "home base" in Phoenix and find another business opportunity that would move me closer to achieving my ultimate goal of building a large company of my own design.

As previously mentioned, from my years in the life insurance business, I learned the art of bringing up objections, and discussing them early on so they are likely to disappear, and most importantly, how the human decision-making process works. It was the beginning of the technique that I refined and what I today call the "Art of Communication." I've used the Art of Communication at every level in my work since I worked for that life insurance company in my mid-20s, and it's been amazingly useful to me. Finance is not my greatest skill; I have been successful at it, but my best assets are that I have a very fertile imagination and I'm a very good communicator and recognize the importance of keeping key relationships. In addition, I was good at using my environment and all the assets around me, and folding them in so that I could get my team and myself where we wanted to go. I wasn't there to memorize a bunch of stuff that didn't mean anything. I stayed focused on my goal. I cared about "How do you get where you want to get?" I knew that I had to continue to build the assets of my Mental Balance Sheet to do that.

Take this opportunity to complete the blank Mental Balance Sheet, filling in the assets I gained and liabilities I acquired based on what you have read thus far about my life and experiences in the life insurance business.

Now compare the assets and liabilities you wrote in the blank Mental Balance Sheet with the assets and liabilities I noted myself for my Mental Balance Sheet after my years working in the life insurance business.

ADDITIONS TO MR. FLEISCHER'S MENTAL BALANCE SHEET 1963-1967 (Life Insurance)

ASSETS	LIABILITIES
Empirical Knowledge:	I *still* didn't know what I didn't know

- The art of negotiation, how to bluff and understanding your opponent
- Direct sales skills
- Know your environment and be prepared so you can accomplish your goals
- Importance of always complying with applicable laws and government regulations
- How life insurance companies can earn money on their liabilities
- Know your environment and be prepared which will enable you to accomplish your goals
- Communicate through asking questions
- How to lead and motivate a sales team
- Intellectual resources and assets make the

difference between success and failure
- The art of becoming a direct salesman and master communicator
- The "take away" strategy I learned in the life insurance business works in many other circumstances
- The art of turning an option on a company into a substantial profit

Intellectual Capital:
- How life insurance companies operate and are financed.
- How actuaries work
    - Statistics and probability

CHAPTER EIGHT – MERGERS AND ACQUISITIONS, SMALL BUSINESS LOANS, AND LAND DEVELOPMENT: HOW AMERICAN BUSINESSES OPERATE (1968-1980)

The business endeavors in which I engaged during the next decade all served as stepping-stones to refine my ultimate goal of creating a large company to my own design which added value to the American economic system. I learned a lot from those businesses, adding significant assets (and in a few instances, liabilities) to my Mental Balance Sheet.

Mergers & Acquisitions (1968-1970)

I was 32 years old with a wife and two children to support when we left Louisiana. After moving back to Phoenix, I read *The Wall Street Journal* every day while thinking about what I wanted to do next. One day, I came across a front-page article about an independent investment banker-type broker named Gil Deakin who worked for himself, and was not associated with any Wall Street investment bank. He put mergers and acquisitions together, earning fees for doing so. I called him and introduced myself, told him my background and he invited me to meet with him.

This meeting led to another helpful asset for the empirical knowledge or personal experience portion of my Mental Balance Sheet: I learned that successful people are often willing to help others who are trying to get started in the business world. It has been my experience that as long as the person asking for help is sincere, respectful and prepared to take action (*i.e.*, not wasting the time of the mentor), the person from whom the help is sought is almost always willing to devote some time and energy to helping a less experienced person succeed by sharing knowledge or advice.

If you remember from our discussion in Chapter Seven, my experiences making direct sales of life insurance, it became clear to me that while making a sales presentation, a useful strategy was to ask the wife of a prospect to get me a drink of water. This tactic resulted in her becoming more interested, and more engaged in the sales presentation, simply because she "helped" me. Meeting with Mr. Deakin taught me that asking for help is useful in other settings as well. As aforementioned, successful members of the business community are often very willing to help and mentor those who are just starting out, by sharing information and strategies that have helped them to become successful.

Mr. Deakin was putting together mergers and acquisitions from his home in Phoenix. A merger happens when two separate companies combine to create a new, joint organization. In contrast, an acquisition occurs when one company (usually larger) takes over, or buys, another company. Generally, the smaller company that is acquired becomes a part of the larger company that buys it, and its assets become part of the larger company. The smaller company often disappears, and no longer exists as a separate entity.

When I met with Mr. Deakin, he showed me how he found private or public companies that needed capital or management, and then found another company that might be an appropriate partner. His leads came from third-party referrals on completed transactions or from the large amount of information that is available about both public and private companies.

I had an acquaintance who was a stockbroker. I talked to him about forming a partnership with me to do mergers and acquisitions, private placements of capital (a private placement is when a group of securities such as stocks are sold through a private offering and is the opposite of a public offering), arrange public offerings or to assist with any other financial needs that our future clients might have. Mr. Deakin agreed to help us and we hung up our shingle: "Fleischer & Fogel – Mergers and Acquisitions, etc." We worked together from 1968 until 1970.

The mid-to-late 1960s was a period of great activity in the American financial world. Conglomerates were the company "du jour". A conglomerate (like General Electric) is a corporation that is made up of a number of different, seemingly unrelated businesses. In a conglomerate, one company owns a controlling stake in a number of smaller companies, which conduct business separately.[1] Mergers were very active. Stocks were rising and many company owners wanted to grow or sell. Our firm, Fleischer & Fogel, focused on the smaller transactions because the big Wall Street houses didn't have much interest in them. The fees they could charge for facilitating the small transactions weren't large enough to make the small deals attractive to the big Wall Street houses; consequently they provided an opportunity for us. An example of this would be a community called Arizona City, which was a land development half-way between Phoenix and Tucson. We arranged a private placement for working capital and took our fees in stock. Later, we arranged for an acquisition of Arizona City by a conglomerate in the south, Fuqua Industries.

We paid a lot of attention to adding value to our clients and had more than modest success in arranging mergers or private placements in the $3-$10 million range, which were "below the radar" of the bigger investment firms. Conducting this business was like having a ticket to a constantly playing movie about how American businesses operate! I talked to or reviewed information about many industries and types of companies, including all different sizes, different organizational structures, and with different forms of ownership, public or private.

The main difference between privately and publicly held companies is that public companies have shares that can be publicly traded on a stock market. A public company has sold a portion of itself to the public by an initial public offering (IPO) of some of its stock, with the result that the shareholders who own that stock have a claim to part of the company's assets and profits. In contrast, privately held companies are usually owned by the company's founders, management, or a small group of private investors.

Public companies, the stocks of which are traded on a U.S. stock exchange, are subject to regulation by the S.E.C.. For example, public companies are generally required to file annual and quarterly financial reports and make other disclosures with the S.E.C. This information is also made available to shareholders and to the public.[2]

The S.E.C. was created shortly after the major stock market crash that occurred in 1929. The government's goal was to restore investor confidence in a financial sector that was notorious for fraudulent activities, unreliable financial and business information and unstable investments. Two major pieces of legislation passed by the U.S. Congress—the Securities Act of 1933 and the Securities Exchange Act of 1934—led to the creation of the S.E.C. and resulted in a regulated financial industry supervised by the government. The goal of both Acts was to protect investors from problems that could arise from fraudulent and questionable activities related to public companies, as well as from dishonest individuals dealing in the securities markets.[3] You may recall that I got my first introduction to the S.E.C. in Chapter 7, when I described how Charlie Sharpe raised funds to capitalize the life insurance company in Louisiana without filing with the S.E.C.. As a result, we had to file a rescission offering, which taught me to make sure that I follow the laws.

The main advantage public companies have is their ability to access the financial markets by selling stock (equity) or bonds (debt) to raise capital (cash) for expansion and projects. The main advantage of remaining a private company is that the management doesn't have to answer to public stockholders and isn't required to file reports with the S.E.C. However, a private company generally can't get financing from the public capital markets and therefore, must turn to private funding to raise money, which can increase the cost of capital and may limit their expansion.[4]

Just because a company is privately held, it isn't necessarily a small company. In actuality, there are many big-name companies that are privately held, such as Cargill, PWC (PriceWaterhouseCoopers), Publix Super Markets, Bechtel, Meijer, and Toys "R" Us,[5] to name a few examples.

While I was involved in mergers and acquisitions, I gained a lot of new assets for my Mental Balance Sheet: I learned about financing techniques, how capital markets and commercial bank finance work; about issuing different types of securities, both debt (bonds) and equity (stocks); how some of the securities laws work (the characteristics of registered and unregistered securities); and I made more than a handsome living from representing others. I also gained a very good education about: business cycles; how Wall Street functions, from the small houses to the big houses; and about how "bubbles" and "greed and fear" are irrational and can cause problems or opportunities when they enter the equation. Consider the following example: prior to 2008, the housing market became significantly overvalued (a bubble) when capital was widely available and people speculated on houses. This drove up their value (greed) until defaults began, sources of financing left, and values dropped rapidly (lack of liquidity caused fear). I learned that these "animal spirits" are endemic to our capitalistic system and are important ingredients that make it function.

It became clear to me that money is made when you create or buy a company, a stock, or a collectible item such as a painting. The crucial point is that you have to buy it at the right value, not at the top of the market (buy low, sell high). I learned that finding a niche that was inefficient, acquiring assets at the right price, and adding value in the form of management and/or capital (thereby increasing value), was a formula that worked and that I could use in the pursuit of my long-term goal.

We made some personal investments in companies and sometimes took stock in lieu of our fees, and as in the Arizona City example, we subsequently arranged for the sale of the company. I found public companies that had emerged from bankruptcy and still had public shareholders. We purchased control, and then merged a private company into the public company which we call a "shell." The private company obtained access to capital, had the public market value its stock, and went public very efficiently. Today it's called a reverse merger.

As I acquired these assets for my Mental Balance Sheet, **my goal of forming a large company to my own design was becoming clearer.** It was becoming apparent to me that finding companies or a niche or business segment that needed financing and capital which the system wasn't providing was where the opportunity I was looking for would be found. I gained a lot of knowledge and experience—valuable assets for my Mental Balance Sheet—during the years my partner and I handled mergers and acquisitions and found the venture to be very rewarding.

Small Business Loans (1970-1973)

While I was still in the mergers and acquisitions business, a gentleman came to our office one day and showed us how his company, located in Los Angeles, provided long-term debt for small companies using the Small Business Administration (SBA) guarantees as a tool. The SBA is a U.S. Government agency that was established in 1953 to promote and strengthen the overall economy by assisting in the establishment and growth of small businesses. SBA loans are term loans from a bank or commercial lending institution for which the SBA guarantees a percentage of the loan principal. The percentage of the loan guaranteed varies based on which SBA financing program (there are several) the loan falls within. SBA guaranteed loans are made by a private lender and guaranteed up to a certain percentage by the SBA, which helps reduce the lender's risk and helps the lender provide financing that's otherwise unavailable at reasonable terms the borrower can afford. The financial markets viewed the small business sector as being too risky for long-term financing, and it would not be available without government guarantees. The SBA guarantee provided a good opportunity for putting together long-term debt financing for small companies.

After we became acquainted, he invited me to join his company as President and run it with him. I liked the opportunity and we got along well, so I accepted his offer, left the mergers and acquisitions business and commuted weekly to Los Angeles while my family stayed in Phoenix. I was highly motivated to do this because I could see that the opportunities for financing and providing long-term debt for small companies were substantial.

We formed a company, found SBA loan prospects, packaged SBA loan packets, and then took them to banks for funding. The market for our services in Los Angeles was very large. There were companies in shopping centers all over Southern California. I developed a plan to create a company that provided long-term financing with SBA guarantees for small businesses. The business model fit my formula due to market size and inefficiency. **It appeared to me that this might be the opportunity that I had been looking for.** The Mental Balance Sheet assets that I had acquired from my work with mergers and acquisitions proved to be very helpful as I pursued this business model.

Following is an example of how this business worked: our sales representatives would call on small manufacturers, retailers, etc. in the Los Angeles area (there were thousands of them) using some of the sales techniques I had learned in the life insurance business. Our sales representatives would explain to the small business owners how we could arrange long-term (4-6 years) debt financing for them. The long-term nature of the financing, as opposed to the short-term financing they then had, would increase the business owner's cash flow because the debt amortization (the amounts of the payments that were due periodically as the debt was paid off) was lower than the amortization to pay off their existing short-term financing. The lower debt payments made it possible for the small businessmen to grow their businesses, because they didn't have to devote as much of their cash flow to making short-term loan payments. An appropriate Current Ratio (the proportion of current assets to current liabilities) for a small business is approximately 2:1, but most of the small companies we approached had a Current Ratio of 1:2. They had too much short-term debt, the payment of which substantially reduced their cash flow. What they needed, and what we were able to help them secure, was a long-term loan in an amount up to $500,000, which would drive their Current Ratio to an appropriate level of 2:1. With a Current Ratio of 2:1, these small businesses were "able to breathe," could create additional positive cash flow, and then grow. Until they were able to change their Current Ratio to 2:1, they had to devote a lot more money to paying back their short-term bank loans quickly; consequently, they didn't have the money necessary to fuel the growth of their companies.

Once our sales representative had located a customer, we would prepare a credit profile package, following Small Business Administration guidelines. We then took the package to a bank and demonstrated for them how our client was credit-worthy. Our proposal was usually that we would provide 90% of the loan, which was guaranteed by the SBA, and the bank would provide 10% of the loan, which was not guaranteed by the government. The 90% of the loan that was guaranteed by the SBA was backed by the "full faith and credit" of the United States government. The government backing meant there would be a large number of investors interested in purchasing the 90% government-guaranteed portion of the loan. The investors would be able to purchase that loan at a "spread" above a U.S. Treasury obligation of similar term (so the loan was a more attractive investment than the U.S. Treasury obligation, which is also backed by the "full faith and credit" of the U.S. government), and below the interest rate the bank received on the loan.

A simplified example of how it works:

1) A loan is made to a business in the amount of $100,000, at an Interest Rate of 9%. The total amount of annual interest that will be paid to the bank in return for the loan will be $9,000.

2) The 90% portion of the loan ($90,000) that's guaranteed by the SBA is sold to an investor at par with a yield of 7%. (For this example I am assuming the amount of the yield is 2% higher than the five-year U.S. Treasury note rate at the time, which would have considerable investor appeal.)

3) The bank is only paying to the investor 7% interest on the guaranteed portion of the overall loan. The bank earns 9% (from the borrower) on its $10,000 advance ($900), plus 2% on the $90,000 portion that was sold to the investor ($1,800).

4) $900 + $1,800 equals $2,700, or 27% return annually on the $10,000 advance. That was a very attractive return on investment for the bank!

5) In addition, the bank had the customers' funds in checking accounts, which had the effect of reducing the bank's investment and further increasing its return.

Using the same example of a $100,000 loan at 9%, another approach is as follows. Rather than continue to hold the guaranteed portion over the life of the loan (as in the prior example) the bank would:

1. Mark up and sell the 90% government guaranteed portion of the loan at a "spread" over treasuries (US Government obligations) with a similar maturity.

2. Assume treasuries were yielding 5% and we sold the guaranteed portion to an investor to yield 7% while the loan was earning 9% on its face. The difference between 9% and 7% (minus the ½% servicing fee to the bank) was our profit.

3. The 90% guaranteed portion was earning $8,100, which is 7.04% of $115,000, minus a servicing fee to the bank of ½%, or $6,250. We could sell the note for $115,000 minus the servicing

fee of $6,250 for $108,750 and have a gross profit of $18,750 ($108,750 minus the $90,000 face amount of the note).

4. In summation, the bank had a onetime gross profit before fees of 187.5% ($18,750 is 187.5% of the banks $10,000 investment in the loan) and an annual return of 9% on the $10,000 (or $900) for the life of the loan.

This was an early form of what is called "securitization" in today's world. It was my introduction to "capital markets," which are "non-bank" sources of capital. The sale of the guaranteed portion of the loan was done through big Wall Street firms like Merrill Lynch or E.F. Hutton. This business opportunity was a great lesson for me on inefficient capital markets. I began to think that we should start doing this ourselves and build our own company, even though we were packaging loans and doing very well. I realized we had an opportunity to pool money to make the loans and use the aforementioned technique to provide returns. We decided to see if we could convince the SBA and others in Washington to create regulations for an entity that we would operate, instead of a bank, to finance SBA loans. In other words, we wanted to create a lender that was not a bank. We contacted several Wall Street investment banks and they indicated that they would help us raise funds if we could get the government to provide regulations for what we labeled a "non-bank lender."

We also needed to get the government to clarify the rules relating to the sale and purchase of the government-guaranteed portion of a loan (90%) so that in the event a buyer bought the note in good faith and the bank discovered fraud or any other form of default, the government would pay the guaranteed portion and go after those parties that might have done something fraudulent, etc. This feature would substantially assist in creating a liquid "secondary market" (*i.e.,* make the investments easier to sell to investors) for the guaranteed portion of the SBA loans. That was essential for our "non-bank" lender to be able to succeed.

The Wall Street firms that I and several other interested parties contacted expressed reservations about our ability to get a license from the SBA for a non-bank lender and get the secondary market rules clarified. However, they told us if we were able to do it, they would capitalize a company for us that would provide small business term loans and we could operate it and own a substantial portion. Once again, **I was thinking this was the opportunity to build a company that I had been searching for**.

As previously mentioned, this was my first introduction to capital markets and my first exposure to securitization. If that is a new term for you, following is a definition:

Securitization is the process of taking an illiquid income-producing asset, or group of assets, and through financial engineering, transforming them into a security. A typical example of securitization is a mortgage-backed security (MBS), which is a type of asset-backed security that is secured by a collection of mortgages on homes or commercial properties. The process works as follows:

First, a regulated and authorized financial institution originates numerous mortgages, which are secured by claims against the various properties the mortgagors purchase. Then, all of the individual mortgages are bundled together into a mortgage pool, which is held in trust as the collateral for an MBS. The MBS can be issued by a third-party financial company, such as a large investment banking firm, or by the same bank that originated the mortgages in the first place. A new security is created, backed up by the claims against the mortgagor's assets, and is divided into "tranches" with the priority of payments and higher rates of return going to those that received payment last and the lower returns to those that receive payments first. This security can be sold to participants in the secondary mortgage market. This market is extremely large, providing a significant amount of liquidity to the group of mortgages, which otherwise would have been quite illiquid on their own.[6]

We believed that if we could do this ourselves—create our own non-bank lender—we could build a company, pool and manage money, which would provide attractive yields to our investors, long term financing which would add value to our customers and as we succeeded, profit for ourselves.

We went to Washington and contacted the SBA and the Federal Reserve indicating our interest in starting a non-bank lending institution. We worked with a very successful man by the name of Jimmy Roosevelt. He was the son of President Franklin D. Roosevelt.

Mr. Roosevelt wrote to Dr. Arthur Burns, who at the time was the head of the Federal Reserve. In the letter, Mr. Roosevelt told Dr. Burns about our idea—we called it the "Small Business Investment Fund of America" (SBIFA) - and said that he wanted to bring me to meet with him. I thought nothing would come of this, but shortly thereafter, Mr. Roosevelt received a letter back from Dr. Burns' secretary that said, "He'd be glad to see you and Mr. Fleischer. Please schedule a meeting at a convenient time." I was scared to death! There I was, a little entrepreneur, and I was going to talk to the second most powerful person in the world, the head of the Federal Reserve, and I was going to make a presentation on how to create further long-term capital for small businesses. Prior to the meeting, I memorized my presentation. After we first arrived, Jimmy Roosevelt and Dr. Burns spent some time reminiscing about President Franklin Roosevelt, but then Dr. Burns turned to me and said, "Well, Mr. Fleischer, tell me why you have come." I was nervous and talked very fast in describing the complexities of the idea. When I finished Dr. Burns looked at me and announced "Mr. Fleischer that sounds very interesting. Now tell me that again, KINDERGARTEN STYLE." Lesson learned: whenever possible, reduce complex ideas to as simple and clean a format as possible. I've used the "kindergarten style" formula many times in my career when attempting clear and succinct communication of ideas or models by me or others. Keep it simple and as logical as possible. I have used and explained the lesson that the Chairman of the Federal Reserve taught me on many occasions, in both my business and personal life.

I learned another valuable lesson when I heard that Mr. Roosevelt talked to President Ford about my idea. There is a definite advantage to taking your proposal to the highest level possible, which you should always try to do. The President of the United States heard about my idea!

Although it seemed like things were on track for the Small Business Investment Fund of America to become a reality, I learned once again (the hard way) that our world is constantly changing. The Watergate scandal became a reality and Washington became "comatose," both before, and for a while after, President Nixon's resignation. We couldn't get anything done and were forced to abandon our plans. I learned an important lesson: to consider very carefully before creating companies that were dependent upon government participation.

Nevertheless, I didn't give up and I persisted in pursuing this business opportunity and running our SBA loan packaging company. After the Watergate furor settled down, the SBA *did* authorize "non-bank" SBA lenders and clarified the secondary market sales for the guaranteed portion as we and others had proposed. Subsequently, the Wall Street investment banks we had talked to also capitalized "non-bank lenders." I heard about it and I went to New York to discuss it with the investment bankers I had originally approached with my idea.

However, when we approached the investment banks concerning our participation in these ventures and reminded them of our meetings when we had first presented the idea and their commitments to work with us, they reneged. Their responses were essentially, "Nice to meet you. We didn't actually think you could do this and do not feel any obligation to you." They had very selective memories and as they were not in writing, declined to keep their agreements. This was a very painful, but also a very clear, lesson: never rely on mid-western handshake values when dealing with people at a certain level (as on Wall Street). From this disappointing experience, I gained some valuable assets for my Mental Balance Sheet. I learned: (1) to reduce agreements to writing; (2) America's capital markets are flexible and can be structured to fill market needs if you are imaginative and persistent enough to do so; and (3) America's financial system (bank and capital markets) is broad and deep.

The government guarantees made it possible for these loans to be created. Initially, inefficient and riskier financial markets require larger profit margins to attract capital, which was the case here. Flash-forward 50 plus years and SBA loan rates have come down, spreads have narrowed (gross profit margins) and the market for the guaranteed portion of SBA loans is robust. We, amongst others, were the leaders in creating this source of funds, which provided long-term debt for small business, which is a major backbone of the American economy. I decided to leave the SBA loan brokerage business and return to Phoenix as it was clear that my long-term goal was unobtainable in this business.

Land Development—Real Estate (1973-1982)

While I was in the mergers & acquisitions business, we arranged a private placement with an investment company for a client who had a 44,000-acre ranch in Northern Arizona. We were paid a fee in stock for the venture. The company was selling 40-acre parcels of land to individuals for recreational homes. The terms of the land sales were 5-10% down with the balance due over 10-15 years. A few years later, about the time I was leaving the small business loan company, the investor called me and said that he had parted ways with the original promoter, saying, "Mort, you got me into this deal. Will you run it?" I agreed to do so. A short time later, this investor ran into personal financial difficulties with his other investments and offered me an opportunity to buy the entire land development company. The price was reasonable and I was able to "boot strap" the purchase (*i.e.*, borrow the purchase price using the assets of the company). I put together the funds to make the purchase price by selling the remaining unsold land to another company in the recreational land sales business and I kept the land contracts receivables for the lots that had been sold previously, which substantially increased my net worth. That was how I made my first million dollars.

A valuable lesson I learned again from this experience: Newton's law applies to business enterprises—things that are in motion tend to stay in motion. In other words, it is sometimes a good idea to find a business that is already up and operating, but may be in trouble, than try to start something from scratch. A great example of this is the life insurance company in Louisiana that I bought with a $5,000 option. It's more difficult to create new companies as the system resists change. I'm not saying you shouldn't start things (I certainly have), especially if you have a fantastic idea—I'm just saying you should give some thought to this theory. It worked for me on a few occasions. It can be harder to start something new rather than fix something that's not running efficiently.

The land sales business assisted me in further refining my moral compass. In our system, there is some leeway as to what a person can represent or negotiate with another. I had concluded that if I didn't believe that I was adding value to the investor, the customer, and therefore to my business, it was not a venture I should pursue. Like all of my other business endeavors, the recreational land sales business added some significant assets to my Mental Balance Sheet. First, I became aware that many Americans love to own land. It's actually part of our culture. Second, I discovered that to be able to sell the recreational land, the payment terms were important and needed to be affordable for the buyers. Third, I learned the value of collateral. If a buyer defaulted on their loan, we took back ownership of the land, and then sold it again to a new party. By financing the buyer's purchase of the land ourselves with a contract, we didn't have to deal with a third-party mortgage on the property and the attendant rights to cure a default that are an inherent part of a mortgage agreement.

However, this endeavor also resulted in some liabilities on my Mental Balance Sheet, and I wasn't comfortable with this business for a number of reasons: (1) the land was remote and for the most part, the buyer never used it; (2) the sales tactics that were employed were very aggressive and didn't fit my moral compass; and (3) I didn't believe in the value-add of the product for the customer. I just didn't really believe that we were selling anything of real value that our customers would use.

Take this opportunity to complete the blank Mental Balance Sheet, filling in the assets I gained and liabilities I acquired based on what you have read thus far about my life and experiences handling mergers and acquisitions, in the Small Business Loans Venture, and in the Land Development enterprise. Now compare the assets and liabilities you wrote in the blank Mental Balance Sheet with the assets and liabilities I noted myself for my Mental Balance Sheet.

ADDITIONS TO MR. FLEISCHER'S MENTAL BALANCE SHEET
(1968-1970) Mergers & Acquisitions,
Small Business Loans and Land Development

ASSETS	LIABILITIES
Empirical Knowledge:	I *still* didn't know what I didn't know

The framework for the "Art of Communication"

- Introduction into utilizing the American Judicial system
- Introduction to "Securitization"
- How some securities laws work
- How business cycles work
- How Wall Street functions
- How "bubbles" and "fear and greed" are irrational and cause problems. Their effects need to be considered separately from a business plan
- Capital markets (non-bank) are broad and deep in America
- Business cycles are inevitable as they are part of our capitalistic system

Moral Compass:

- I was uncomfortable selling something (land) that many people would never use

CHAPTER NOTES

[1]*Ibid.*

[2]*Investopedia.* "What's the Difference Between Publicly – and Privately-held Companies?" http://www.investopedia.com. Accessed January 10, 2016.

[3]*Investopedia.* "Policing the Securities Market: An Overview of the S.E.C.." http://www.investopedia.com/articles/02/112202.asp#ixzz3y14cCvZw. Accessed January 10, 2016.

[4]*Investopedia.* "What's the Difference Between Publicly – and Privately-held Companies?" http://www.investopedia.com. Accessed January 10, 2016.

[5]*Forbes.com.* "The Largest Private Companies." 11.09.06. http://www.forbes.com. Accessed January 10, 2016.

[6]Gallant, Chris. *Investopedia.*"What is Securitization?" http://www.investopedia.com/ask/answers/07/securitization.asp#ixzz3yQPStCzt. Accessed January 10, 2016

CHAPTER NINE – ADVENTURES IN A NEW ENVIRONMENT AND UNDERSTANDING THE LIMITS OF MY RISK TOLERANCE: THE COAL MINE YEARS (1973-1977)

There are times in each of our lives when we experience events that are so impactful, that teach us so much that they become life-changing, life-defining experiences. Meeting a man by the name of Robert Halliday was the beginning of such an experience for me. He was quite instrumental in helping me build significant assets for my Mental Balance Sheet.

The first time I met Bob it was impossible not to be impressed by him. He was a large and imposing Scotsman at 6'5" tall, weighing 250 pounds and was very tough. He had been a frogman in WWII and was part of the D-Day invasion on Omaha Beach. He was wounded in battle many times while on active duty and received seven Purple Hearts.[1] One of his wounds was a serious head injury. Doctors were able to "put him back together," placing a metal plate in his head, but it took him two long years to learn to speak again. Despite such a severe injury, Mr. Halliday fought his way back to recovery and had a very successful business career, as he was a very strong and motivated man. He worked as a CPA for the prestigious national accounting firm Arthur

Anderson, then moved to his hometown of Boise, Idaho in 1956 where he built a career with Boise Cascade.[2]

> According to the University of Idaho Foundation, [Mr. Halliday] became known as particularly astute in financial problem solving and decision making as [Boise Cascade's] vice president, treasurer and director. He was known as the "brains behind dizzying growth and acquisitions of the company . . . ." He also led the merger of environmental service and manufacturing company Wheelabrator-Frye; and helped launch Franchise Finance Corporation and the vast and self-sufficient Nevada IL Ranch, among numerous other enterprises."[3]

When I first encountered Bob Halliday, I was in the mergers and acquisitions business, and he was the Chairman-CEO of Wheelabrator-Frye and U.S. Natural Resources, both public companies. In the beginning, I worked with him when I was running Fleischer and Fogel to put together mergers. Later, I worked for him, and eventually we became partners. We were together for 30-plus years. He liked to find what he thought were talented young men, train them and become partners with them in a venture. I had stayed in close touch with Bob while I was in the Small Business loans venture. In 1973, after I had left that business, I received a call from Bob Halliday, inviting me to come to Boise to "work with him on deals." He was a highly intelligent man—he actually memorized the tax code. But if ever there was a pirate, it was Bob. He loved to buy things and boot strap-finance them. He was a real "deal junkie" and a hard taskmaster, and I loved him. So I jumped at the chance to work with him. He became my mentor and taught me so much. I "attended" what I like to call the "Halliday MBA School." He took me with him to Wall Street banking firms. I noticed immediately that everybody treated him with the utmost respect, continually responding to his requests with, "Yes Sir, Mr. Halliday!" He had an aura about him that commanded respect. My Master Adaptive Learner training immensely helped me to progress to a higher level of learning ability and to realize additional potential for achievement under his tutelage.

While I was in Bob's office one day, he pointed out that coal prices were increasing substantially and suggested that we should put a coal mine together. I agreed and thought it might be a good idea, even though I knew ZERO about the coal mining world. Bob reached into his desk, took out a check and made it out to me for $1,000,000! Then he said, "Go to Alabama and buy a coal mine." I did just that. I found a company and boot strapped the purchase of a coal mine that we named "Southern States Coal." We only purchased 75% of the company, leaving the seller with a 25% interest. We then used the seller's assets, equipment and coal reserves to collateralize a loan and borrow the purchase price of $5 million.

I probably learned more from that coal mining business than anything else I did in my entire business career. It was a tremendous lesson in being a Master Adaptive Learner, and the experience provided major assets for building my Mental Balance Sheet. For one thing, I began to understand the difference between rational academic risk assessment and emotional risk tolerance. **Everyone needs to determine and constantly be aware of what his personal risk tolerance is.** Understanding the limits of your risk tolerance makes it easier to sleep at night. I had occasion to further refine my moral compass, and had more than one difficult encounter to test the depth of my character, as I'll describe.

Birmingham, Alabama is at the southern end of the Appalachian Mountains, and Southern States Coal owned a strip mine nearby. The strip mine contained two types of coal reserves: (1) steam or "thermal" coal and (2) metallurgical coal. Steam coal, which is lower in carbon content and calorific value, is the world's most abundant fossil fuel and is primarily used to produce energy. Metallurgical coal is less abundant than thermal coal and is primarily used in the production of coke, which is an important part of the steel milling process.[4] Southern States Coal had just two customers: Alabama Power, which purchased the steam coal, and U.S. Steel, which needed the metallurgical coal. Unfortunately, neither Alabama Power nor U.S. Steel paid us on time. As a result, it wasn't long before I came to understand the problems and I realized I needed to use receivables financing to mitigate some of our cash flow difficulties. I had to quickly learn how to finance accounts receivable and I was able to convince an Alabama bank to lend us money secured by them.

To make a challenging situation even more difficult, I also realized I was completely unfamiliar with the Southern culture and business practices of Alabama. I knew that I needed a partner who "spoke Alabamese." While we were structuring the acquisition, I proposed that the person who had introduced Bob Halliday and me to the seller and who knew the coal mining industry make an investment in the company, as I thought he would become a valuable partner who knew the local environment. He agreed to invest, and the resulting ownership structure was that the seller retained 25%, the local businessman invested and acquired 25%, and Bob Halliday and I each owned 25% of the company. We borrowed the purchase price against the coal reserves, the equipment such as the draglines (they are huge, 10-story tall, earth-moving machines) and front-end loaders. As previously discussed, "boot strap financing" is when an entrepreneur starts a company with little capital. The entrepreneur attempts to find and finance the purchase of a company by borrowing against the operating revenues, net cash flow and assets such as equipment and coal reserves of the company.

That coal mine was constantly in financial difficulty, partly because it was undercapitalized. During my career, it was one of the few businesses in which we lost money. Coal mining is a risky business. It is subject to fluctuating commodity prices (coal), management intensive, capital-intensive, labor intensive, and regulatory intensive. I would learn that these variables are difficult to manage, particularly in a thinly capitalized company with little room for error.

The intensive involvement of unions, primarily the United Mine Workers (UMW) and Teamsters Unions, further complicated operating the coal mine. I learned "the hard way" that when you make a contract with the UMW or the Teamsters, they may not abide by it. The next day, if they "don't like" the contract, they simply won't honor it or will honor only the part that they like. The overriding principle that I learned, which was a tremendous asset for my Mental Balance Sheet, was that **contracts are only as good as the people behind them**.

At a time when the company was short on cash, our Alabama partner approached me one day and said that the Teamsters Union would loan us money. An individual who said that he represented Jimmy Hoffa and the Teamsters (which turned out to be untrue) came to see me and told me, "You give us a finder's fee Mort, and we'll get you a good loan." I called Bob Halliday and told him, "We're really short of money, we'd better do this." I gave them the finder's fee and got *nothing* in return; it was a scam and a fraud. But I learned a valuable lesson: not to deal with shady characters misrepresenting their connection to the Teamsters' assets to make money for themselves. I got a "big dose" of dealing with unions, and learned that the very nature of unions makes a few of them susceptible to corruption. A small group controls much of the members' money. It was a valuable asset for my Mental Balance Sheet, recognizing the challenges that arise from dealing with people of questionable morals.

My time at Southern States Coal provided another powerful example of that lesson when I was approached by two men from Alabama Power. They walked into my office one day and announced, "We know that we and U.S. Steel are your only two customers, Mort, and we're not going to buy any more coal from you unless you pay us off personally." The price of coal at this time was going up rapidly, which fueled a lot of greed and short-term thinking, which sometimes prompts persons with lower values to try and make "fast money." I was so angry, I immediately responded, "Get the *&@! out of my office!" They didn't know what to do. They were completely shocked—nobody ever talked to them that way! So they left. Somehow they figured out that Bob Halliday was my partner, and Bob's company, Wheelabrator Frye controlled Rust Engineering in Birmingham. So they got themselves down to Rust Engineering, and the boys there called Bob Halliday. It wasn't long before I received a call from Bob asking me, "What are you doing down there? Throwing guys out?" I confirmed for him, "They wanted payoffs and I threw them out." Bob responded, "You've got to operate with less visibility, Mort! We can't run that coal mine if they don't want to buy anything from us. You need to move so that they don't know where you are!" So I had to leave town. From that time on, I flew into the airport once a week, and my staff would meet me there and we'd conduct our meetings at the airport. I'd find out how the Company was doing, tell the staff what I wanted them to do, and remain in hiding.

One day I received an unexpected phone call from a government lawyer who told me that a Grand Jury was being convened. The government was planning to indict the Alabama Power men for taking payoffs, and needed Bob Halliday and me to appear before the Grand Jury. We were both subpoenaed, even though Bob Halliday had nothing to do with the day-to-day operations of the coal mine. He needed to be there because he was a major shareholder in Southern States Coal—the victim.

During the Grand Jury investigation, as I sat on the stand testifying, the government's attorney asked me, "Mr. Fleischer, do you see anybody in this courtroom who ever asked you for payoffs?"

And I responded, "Yes, those two guys right over there," as I pointed at the Alabama Power boys. They were indicted and went to jail. I learned that the American justice system works. Maybe even more importantly, I once again learned that I was right to stick to the courage of my convictions, and stay true to my own moral character. When I refused to pay the Alabama Power boys their payoffs, I made it clear to them that I wasn't a "good ol' boy," and I wasn't going to "play along" with them. If I had caved in and paid them off that first time that they asked, they undoubtedly would have kept coming back for more. Regardless, I knew they wouldn't stop buying coal from me, because they knew I'd "holler." They knew they'd have to kill me to stop me from talking, which was always a distinct possibility, but I didn't think they were that brave. They were greedy, short term, immoral men.

When the Grand Jury indicted those two, I was back in business. The local southern businessmen were embarrassed by the situation; they didn't want that kind of activity happening in their community.

Another challenge while running Southern States Coal was learning in a shocking way that coal can be a volatile commodity. I had decided to speculate on some of the coal, because the price was going up rapidly. I stored the coal in a large pile on the ground, and it caught on fire as the result of spontaneous combustion, destroying an asset and future cash flow. Yet another difficulty with the coal mining business is that it requires a lot of equipment maintenance. The equipment that we purchased with the company was defective and we spent a huge amount of money constantly repairing it.

The coal mining enterprise also taught me about "take-or-pay" contracts. With that type of contract, a big company with really good credit would agree to pay our coal company for our coal, even if they didn't "take" it. With a big enough take-or-pay contract, I could use it to finance our company. I could take that contract to a bank, as it showed that our customer had agreed to buy coal and pay us for it even if they didn't take it. I could borrow money utilizing the larger company's credit, which we could use to operate our coal mine company.

As I've indicated, Southern States Coal was undercapitalized and lacked adequate cash to operate. It constantly had financial troubles and a take-or-pay contract would have been a valuable resource. The coal purchasing companies were willing to sign a take-or-pay contract because they wanted an assured supply of coal at a fixed price that would allow them to run their plants profitably with greater certainty. They wanted to mitigate against the risk of the price of coal rising. Alternatively, they could have speculated in the "spot market"—the market where a buyer can purchase coal on an *ad hoc* basis. But no buyer wanted to do that for its entire coal supply; if the price of coal went up substantially, their margins would have been harmed. So they were willing to sign take-or-pay contracts and lend their credit to assure a basic supply of coal at an affordable price. We were willing to enter into the take-or-pay contract as it would have made our small company credit-worthy, provide an opportunity for working capital loans and lead to profitability. We didn't intend to put all of our mining production under take-or-pay contracts, because if the price of coal rose we could sell the balance of our mining production in the "spot" markets for a higher price. I was negotiating with both a Japanese and a German company; unfortunately we did not stay in the business long enough for the transactions to be completed. Had we obtained those contracts, our outcome in Southern States Coal may have been different.

One of the more unexpected challenges of the coal-mining venture arose from the Alabama culture in which we were operating. Many of the men signed their names by writing an "X" on the signature line. In many instances, they were illiterate, with little educational background. Our coal company was a "strip mine," that is, the coal seam is close enough to the surface that explosives would be utilized to loosen the overburden (dirt) above the seam which then enabled the draglines and front end loaders to remove the dirt above the coal and then pick up the coal from the uncovered seam. Drilling holes for the explosives in the top soil over the coal seam was a difficult art form that required the skills of an engineer, and the coal seams were often damaged by the explosive concussion destroying a portion of the coal. These same uneducated people were often in charge of this process, and our results were often mixed. I hired several different external "Consultants" to assist, however our results were still marginal. Lesson Learned: professional, well-trained, knowledgeable people are important.

Another example of the unexpected challenges caused by the Alabama culture occurred one day when I went down to the mine with the mine manager. He was drinking white lightning (homemade whiskey with carbon in the bottom) from the glove compartment in his truck, which was a common practice in Alabama. As we arrived at the mine, one of the huge mining trucks drove up out of the mine pit, loaded with coal. It was a contract truck, not a truck that we owned, and as it got to the top of the pit, it stalled. A man jumped out, pulled out his .45 caliber pistol and BANG! BANG! BANG! BANG! shot up the carburetor in the truck's engine through the hood. I asked the Mine manager, who knew the guy, to go ask him why he had done that. When the Manager approached and asked him, "Why are you doing that?" his reply was, "I'm getting the debbils out of our trucks." In Alabama, "debbil" is how some our mine employees pronounced "devil." He blew the carburetor away because he believed there were devils in it. That was another example of the intellect level of some of the men working at that mine, which of course, presents its own set of problems when trying to run such an operation.

On another occasion when we visited the mine, we discovered a worker sitting on the fuel dump, smoking a cigarette. At a fuel dump, there is always the danger of leaking or spilled fuel. Front end loaders, drag lines, and other equipment utilize the fuel dump. Yet this employee was sitting on the fuel dump, smoking a lighted cigarette. The Mine manager screamed at him, "You stupid #$%*! What are you doing? This thing could explode and blow you into eternity!" The employee remained unfazed.

Still another ever present danger were highwall accidents. When the overburden (dirt) is removed over a coal seam, there is a "high wall" adjacent to the coal seam that is often times left. Sometimes an employee would drive a front end loader or tractor next to the high wall and it would partially collapse and fall in on him. We'd have to rush him to the hospital. These types of risks were difficult to control and quantify.

It was becoming clear to me that the coal mine was a venture that might fail. The commodity (fluctuating) price of coal and the thin (undercapitalized) balance sheet along with many other variables made the company's chances for success highly questionable. Consequently, Bob Halliday and I agreed that we should close the company. He was tired of providing the shortfall (deficit financing) for the cash requirements as the company was losing money. I couldn't blame him.

When we bought the company, Mr. Halliday personally signed and guaranteed a note for $5,000,000, which as you'll recall we borrowed from a bank in Birmingham. Our challenge was to get the bank to release him from that guaranty obligation, so if the company's assets were sold but didn't bring enough proceeds to repay the bank the $5,000,000, Bob would not have to pay the shortfall as his personal guarantee would require him to do.

As I mentioned, the seller had retained 25% ownership of company. He had misrepresented the condition of a lot of the equipment and our maintenance costs were high. During the time I ran the coal mine, I would occasionally shoot pool with the seller at his home, and he would brag about how he was not truthful with the IRS regarding his earnings and taxes due. I reached into my Mental Balance Sheet and remembered how Charlie Sharpe dealt with the state of Louisiana when we were requesting a license renewal. I took the seller to lunch and refreshed his memory regarding Mr. Halliday's guaranty to the Birmingham bank for the $5,000,000, which was used to pay the purchase price. I *strongly* suggested that he go to the bank and get Bob

Halliday removed from his personal guaranty and assume the note. The incentive for him doing so was that we would convey to him 75% of the stock and he would then own the company again. In light of the faulty equipment he sold us and the coal reserve misrepresentations he had made when negotiating the sale of the company, I made it clear to him that if he didn't do as I requested we were considering suing him or we might go to the IRS and suggest they talk to him about his tax returns.

I really didn't know anything about his taxes, other than what I heard him briefly allude to while shooting pool. However, the strategy worked and very shortly thereafter the bank called Mr. Halliday and told him that he was relieved of his responsibility on the notes he had guaranteed. We delivered 75% of the common stock back to the original seller and essentially sold the company back to him.

The coal-mining venture was the business that I probably learned the most from in my entire career as it provided major assets for building my Mental Balance Sheet. I further refined my moral compass and had more than one difficult occasion to test the depth of my character. When all was said and done, we lost several million dollars in the coal mining venture, but in retrospect, I think it was money well-invested. I learned so much from the experience; about a venture that was management intensive, capital intensive, labor intensive, regulatory intensive, and union intensive, and since coal is a commodity, it is subject to substantial price fluctuations.

I learned another big lesson as I began to clearly define for myself and understand the difference between academic modeling variables and projections, risk assessment, and emotional risk tolerance. I define "emotional risk tolerance" as your ability to tolerate the emotions that occur when dealing with many variables you cannot control. Projecting the financial results we could have expected to obtain from operating the coal mine was relatively easy. However, everyone needs to determine what level of emotional risk they want to tolerate when analyzing a business venture or job. You will sleep better at night.

ADDITIONS TO MR. FLEISCHER'S MENTAL BALANCE SHEET (1973-1976) The Coal Mine

ASSETS	LIABILITIES
Empirical Knowledge:	I *still* didn't know what I didn't know
• Coal mining is very risky, particularly with a thinly capitalized company	
• Difference between quantitative risk (projections) and emotional risk tolerance (ability to sleep at night)	

CHAPTER NOTES

[1]2003-2004 Annual Report, University of Idaho Foundation, Inc., p.6.
[2]*Ibid.*
[3]*Ibid.*
[4]www.gccoal.com, November 12, 20

CHAPTER TEN – REFINING MY GOALS—THE HISPANIC RADIO STATION (1978-1979)

After Bob Halliday and I sold the coal mining business, I returned to Phoenix, which was always my home base. A mutual banking friend introduced me to a Mexican businessman who was interested in purchasing one of the two existing Hispanic radio stations in Phoenix. He believed (and after review, I agreed) that the Hispanic population was rapidly expanding in the U.S. and there was an opportunity to start in Phoenix with a radio station. We believed we could show the overall market the existing and future buying power of the Hispanic population in the U.S. I recognized that if I could have a Mexican partner, much like I had needed the Alabama partner in the coal mine, we could then either buy or eventually create a chain of radio stations around the periphery of the country, where the Hispanic populations were concentrated. We undertook this venture at a time when a Hispanic radio station was for sale in town. We believed we could buy the station, show the Anglo community the expanding market, broaden the advertising and the listener base, and I thought it could be an exciting venture. I could envision the possibility of owning a chain of Hispanic radio stations. We could use my knowledge of the SBA system to get a loan for $375,000, and then make up the balance of the $700,000 purchase price by obtaining a bank loan and contributing cash (equity).

The Mexican businessman came from a prominent, well-known Mexican family: his Father owned a large liquor distribution business in Mexico, and his sister was a well-known television newscaster. I realized his family's strong personal reputation would be helpful to us in arranging financing to purchase the radio station in Phoenix. We made a deal pursuant to which we agreed to pay $700,000 for the station. I used my knowledge of SBA loans (a valuable asset on my Mental Balance Sheet) and arranged an SBA loan for $375,000. The balance of the purchase price would be made up of a bank loan for $200,000, plus $200,000 of equity ($125,000 and $75,000 working capital to run the station). Our business plan was to develop our marketing strategy focusing on key national clients in Phoenix that we could then service both locally and more broadly as we developed our chain of Hispanic radio stations.

I found operating the radio station interesting and was particularly intrigued by the opportunity to build or acquire more stations across the U.S., wherever the Hispanic population was growing. I had called on my Mental Balance Sheet and used my knowledge in finance and dealing with government regulations to structure the purchase, obtain an SBA loan, and comply with the Federal Communications Commission (FCC) rules. The quasi-monopolistic characteristics of radio station licensing by the government had the potential to increase the value of the stations, because the entry of competitors into the market is restricted. The FCC limits the number of licenses it will issue, and it has strict regulations as to who can qualify to obtain such a license. The value of the stations would also increase if revenue was increasing due to the expanding Hispanic market. Marketing, sales, and management (intellectual capital) were the key.

I have to say it was at best "'sort of exciting.'" I liked the business and it seemed okay, but after a time, I realized it was a very small niche. Although my foray into the world of broadcasting was to be fairly short-lived, I still gained some valuable assets for my Mental Balance Sheet. I learned about the communications industry, advertising and how revenues from advertising, fund the operation of a radio station. I also learned about the "quasi-monopoly" value created by government licensing of a radio station, which when properly managed, restricts the ease of entry of competitors and thereby increases the value of the operating station. Remember, this was before the Internet, Internet radio and cable television. Radio stations were then a type of monopoly.

Take this opportunity to complete the blank Mental Balance Sheet, filling in the assets I gained and liabilities I acquired based on what you have read thus far about my life and experiences running the Hispanic radio station.

Next, compare the assets and liabilities you wrote in the blank Mental Balance Sheet with the assets and liabilities I noted for myself in my Mental Balance Sheet after my experiences running the Hispanic radio station.

ADDITIONS TO MR. FLEISCHER'S MENTAL BALANCE SHEET (1978-1979) The Hispanic Radio Station

ASSETS	LIABILITIES
Empirical Knowledge:	I *still* didn't know what I didn't know

Empirical Knowledge:

- The value of government licensing
- Learned about the basics of the communications industry
- Advertising essentially funds the operations of a radio station

CHAPTER ELEVEN – LUCK IS WHEN OPPORTUNITY MEETS PREPAREDNESS: SINGLE-TENANT REAL ESTATE FINANCE (1979-PRESENT)

In mid-1979 when I was 43 years old, I received a call from a man who ran the real estate development department for a fast food restaurant chain. He arranged a meeting with me at my office at the radio station, where he told me that he had heard that I had a "fertile imagination" and his chain needed capital to finance real estate for their franchisee restaurants. Their business opportunity was large, but they could not generate capital fast enough from operations to finance the real estate necessary to house their restaurants and meet the demand for new locations. I did some research into the fast food restaurant industry and could see that it was growing very rapidly. It appeared to me that a good operator with a new fast food restaurant and a decent brand, who built their restaurant in a reasonably good location, had an excellent chance for success. Looking around the country, it became pretty clear that the restaurant franchise industry was a really big business. Fast food restaurants were everywhere and expanding. Not only was the industry large, there were also very big growth opportunities. I talked to some local commercial bankers I knew, but they didn't want to finance restaurant real estate because the franchisees, in many instances, were under-capitalized and inexperienced. The bankers deemed it just too risky.

It appeared to me that this was a tremendous opportunity and if I could create a financial model that would work and if I could find a source of capital for the real estate, it may be the opportunity I had been searching for so many years! The operators of these fast food restaurants were "little guys"; they were classic American entrepreneurs. When I met with them, they frequently provided me with their financial statements written on napkins. **I knew I was going to need to create a new credit model** in order to get the financing necessary to make this new venture work.

A New Credit Model

In considering how to formulate a credit model that would work, I realized I would have to partially "forget" about the way commercial bankers were viewing this business sector when they decided whether to extend credit. Today I would call their approach "top-down financing" because the banks considered the franchisee's profit/loss statement and balance sheet (their basic financial statements) in making the determination of whether the franchisee was creditworthy. The banks denied the application for credit if a decision was reached that the franchisee's financial situation was inadequate to support advancing funds for real estate, which was many times the case.

We called the new credit model that we created "bottom-up credit." Our current company, STORE Capital still uses this basic model, and after 39 years in the business, we have used the bottom-up credit model to finance almost 9,600 properties, investing $17 billion through four different companies that we created that originally financed restaurant real estate. We have expanded it into many different categories which we now call "Single-tenant Real Estate."

In a bottom-up credit model, when deciding whether to extend credit to a fast food restaurant operator, we considered different factors than the commercial banks considered using their traditional "top-down" financing model. Simply stated our model is:

First: don't advance (pay) more than the replacement cost for the real estate. In the event that the operator fails, we can re-rent it to another operator at an affordable rent.

Second: look at every location as an individual profit center. Determine how much cash flow the operator has available to pay the lease or mortgage payment (we added this step later).

Third: review their profit and loss statements and balance sheet. Most importantly, consider the operator's character and credit track record.

We call this model "bottom-up credit" analysis. The credit is inherent in the real estate itself. By not advancing more than the replacement cost of the real estate itself, we didn't overpay. We view each unit as a profit center rather than being unpleasantly surprised if 20% of the units can produce 80% of the cash flow and we've consequently purchased a lot of marginal locations. Our sources of payment are:

a. The unit level profitability—each unit has its own profit and loss statement which is our primary source

b. If the asset we invest in fails to produce profit, then payments are received from cash flow of other corporate assets

c. Underlying real estate value; either sell or re-let the unit

The name of our first company was "Franchise Finance Company of America" (FFCA). We utilized a sales-leaseback structure to finance the real estate. In other words, we purchased and owned the land, building, and equipment, and then leased them back to the franchisee. Almost all of our franchisees wanted an option to own the real estate, so we generally provided them an option to buy the real estate after 15-20 years. At most, only 1% of the franchisees have ever purchased the real estate. This was largely because they didn't have the capital to buy the real estate at the outset, and after another 15 years, they still didn't have it—because they were smarter operators and had used their capital to invest in operations and grow their businesses, not invest in real estate where returns on equity are lower. The biggest challenge for us at FFCA was always how to teach business operators that owned real estate about return on equity. A dollar of cash flow from operations is worth more than a dollar invested in real estate. Our franchisees were not in the real estate business, they were in the business of operating restaurants. The franchisees that grasped this concept and understood sale-leasebacks were generally extremely successful. At the risk of being repetitive, return on equity from the restaurant operations was much larger than that from the real estate. The true value of this kind of "profit center" real estate to most business owners is the amount of cash flow toward the business operating profit it will produce.

We decided that as a business practice, FFCA managed partnerships would own the real estate and equipment debt-free, to further mitigate risk. We did not want to burden the partnerships we managed with debt. One of the benefits of this was that if we needed to take a property back because a franchisee defaulted on his lease payments, we didn't have to go talk to a lender. When a franchisee had financial difficulties, we had to decide if he was part of the solution or part of the problem. When a franchisee defaulted on his lease payments, FFCA would take back the property, terminate the lease and then lease it to a different operator. We didn't have to deal with foreclosing a mortgage and all the complexities that accompany that process. It was much more efficient to re-lease the property to a new operator or sell it. This idea was the basis of "bottom-up credit" and our model has worked very well. We believe that our loss of investment capital from investing in this asset class have approximately than 2% over 39 years, which is an enviable record.

The key was not only having good operators (it didn't matter if the operator was new in the fast food restaurant business, as long as he was a good operator). Having a first-class location and a good brand were also crucial. If we thought the consumer identified with the brand (known as strong "brand equity") and as long as the franchisee put "value on the plate" (*i.e.*, good food), the restaurant would normally prosper and be able to pay the rent due under the lease. "Brand equity" refers to the value or consumer recognition of a brand. If a consumer is aware of a brand and associates good qualities with it, such as high product quality, then the consumer is likely to buy (and continue buying) that brand. A few examples of fast food companies with great brand equity are McDonald's, Hardee's, Arby's, Burger King, and Taco Bell. The consumer is familiar with those brands and knows the quality of the product and its price and value when he visits those restaurants, unlike the first time he visits an unknown restaurant.

After considering the replacement value of the real estate and unit level cash flow, we put a lot of emphasis on the experience, motivation and character of the operator. Did he understand the importance of putting "value on the plate," *i.e.,* good food? A good operator can prosper in a secondary location while a poor operator sometimes failed even with a superior location. Our credit model is different than that of many banks and as you'll see, afforded us an extraordinary opportunity.

Perception vs. Reality

It was my opinion that we could raise real estate capital, become asset and real estate managers, and fill a large need in what was clearly a rapidly growing inefficient market: the financing of the real estate for fast food restaurants. I presented my idea to my mentor, Mr. Halliday (whom, as you'll recall I had known from my time arranging mergers and acquisitions, SBA loans and the coal mine) and he loved it. He was friendly with the Chairman of the board of E. F. Hutton, a large Wall Street investment firm, which at the time had 8,000 brokers (like Merrill Lynch). I also knew the people at E. F. Hutton from my SBA days (selling the guaranteed portions of small business loans as investments) and the coal mine operation. The people at E. F. Hutton also liked my idea; but even though they thought my "bottom-up credit" financing model would work, they believed that to make the investment attractive to public investors, they would need to insure the lease payments with an outside insurance company, because of the perceived "weak" franchisee credit.

At this point it became very apparent to me that in the financial world, there is **"reality," and there is "perception."** The factor that impacts potential investors in addition to reality is "perception." E. F. Hutton's goal was to make the investment appealing as possible to investors, so its brokers could sell it without great difficulty. If the public **perceived** that a franchisee's credit was weak, people would have been reluctant to invest in the partnership. E. F. Hutton's solution to this problem was to suggest that I find an insurance company that would insure the operator's lease payments (if the operator failed to make his lease payments, the insurance would kick in and make the payment). As I will discuss, I found such a company and we eventually called our investment product "Insured Income Properties." The insurance made the investment more marketable for a broker to sell to an investor. When a broker presented the investment to a potential investor, he could build the investor's confidence by telling him that the cash flow was "insured by a big insurance company." We quit using the insurance once we had enough assets under management that consistently performed, and the market could see that our credit model worked.

Creating Opportunities

Because E. F. Hutton was requiring lease payment insurance to underwrite everything, my next challenge became finding an insurance company that would provide the lease payment insurance. I called Best's, an insurance rating company that I knew from my life insurance company days (using the assets of my Mental Balance Sheet). The people at Best's knew of an insurance company in the South that financed SBA loans, and suggested that company might also be interested in insuring franchisee lease payments that were backed up by my "bottom-up credit" model, with good fast food chains (strong brand equity) and skilled operators.

I located the phone number of the President of the insurance company recommended by Best's, called him and told his secretary that I had a great opportunity for their company, and that they were "first on my list," but if I didn't get to meet with him, I would have to go elsewhere (using the "take it away" strategy that I learned from my life insurance sales days). You can see how my Mental Balance Sheet assets were helping me. The secretary put me through to the company President immediately. As we spoke, he told me that he was awfully busy getting ready for a trip the next day. I asked if I could meet with him in the airport prior to his flight, in order to conserve his time. I persuaded him that he would want to hear about this great opportunity and that I too was pressed for time (take it away—create urgency). He agreed to meet with me. I was in Phoenix and flew to North Carolina **that day** so I could meet with him in the airport before he left town. It was a successful meeting. He understood my proposal, obviously knew of E. F. Hutton (which helped give my proposal credibility), and he liked my "bottom-up credit" concept and formula. He compared it to the SBA-type of financing his insurance company had been providing. We agreed on the price for insuring the franchisees' lease payments, wrote it on a napkin, shook hands mid-western style, and he agreed to insure 80% of the lease payments on the real estate (building and land). After calling Mr. Halliday with the great news, I took the next plane to New York to talk to E. F. Hutton.

This experience added a great new asset to my Mental Balance Sheet: because I was persistent, and thought creatively, I was able to devise an opportunity where one otherwise wouldn't have existed. If I had waited until the busy President of the insurance company decided he had time to meet with me, our meeting might never have happened. By presenting the idea that we could meet at the airport (an unorthodox approach), I was being considerate of his time and busy schedule, I provided a much more appealing opportunity (from the president's perspective) for us to meet. I also was prepared and able to make the meeting happen quickly, in accordance with my timing preferences.

My meeting in New York with the people at E. F. Hutton was equally successful. With the lease rental payments insured, E. F. Hutton agreed to underwrite raising the funds to finance single-tenant restaurant real estate. They suggested we use a limited partnership format to own the real estate, with a management company to manage the partnership assets. It was important to me that I controlled the management company. When a person owns 51% of something, from a control perspective, it's essentially the same as owning 100%. I knew from my Wall Street days (once again I drew from the assets of my Mental Balance Sheet) that if I was going to undertake this venture, spend a lot of time working on it, and build a substantial company, I needed to have the last word on decisions—because you never know what will happen—and 51% ownership gave me the last and controlling word. So the management company was formed, and we called it "Franchise Finance Corporation of America" (FFCA). FFCA was owned 51% by me, 24% by Mr. Halliday, and 25% by E. F. Hutton. The result of having E. F. Hutton's involvement was that FFCA had instant recognition and the potential to have 8,000 of their stock brokers raising capital for us to manage and invest in restaurant real estate.

Finding and Fulfilling My Ultimate Goal

I returned to Phoenix, very excited and believing that I had **finally found the opportunity that would fulfill my long-term goal** of building a large company of my own design that added value. I immediately began to negotiate the sale of my interest in the Hispanic radio station to my partners, as I wanted to be able to focus full-time on building our new company and **accomplishing my goal**. The radio station opportunity was not big enough to be consistent with my long-term goal. The opportunity to finance "single-tenant" restaurant real estate was a **big opportunity in an inefficient financial market**.

I called the fast food restaurant chain that had originally approached me for real estate financing. Surprisingly, when I informed them that we were ready to provide financing for the real estate for their franchisee-owned restaurants, they declined the opportunity (foolishly, in my opinion) because they thought it was "too risky."

However, E. F. Hutton moved forward and sent a letter to a group of fast food restaurant chains, informing them that we were prepared to raise capital for sale-leaseback real estate financing for franchisee operated restaurants, and suggesting that if they had interest to call me. Within several days of receiving that letter, Hardee's (a large southern fast food chain) called me and said they liked the idea. They saw the need for the service and assets we would provide, and our first prospectus for Hardee's Lease Partners was prepared and underwritten by E. F. Hutton. I happily sold my interest in the Hispanic radio station to my partners and went into this business full-time.

Single-tenant Real Estate

I knew this was the large opportunity I had been seeking and for which I had been **preparing my Mental Balance Sheet my entire life.** Single-tenant restaurant real estate was a large, inefficient finance market that was growing rapidly due to the rapid growth of the fast food industry. Our "bottom-up credit" model mitigated our risk, and we could add value to our investors as well as to our franchisee customers. **Adding value** to investors (equity holders) and customers (users of capital) **should be a primary mission if a business is to succeed.** THIS PRINCIPLE IS A PREREQUISITE TO MAKING LONG TERM PROFITS! Some people create business enterprises and may use financial engineering and short-term goals, only to make money without adding long term value. They may succeed, but it is more likely that they won't. It has been my observation that people who work to add value have a much greater chance of success, and a much better "journey" along the way. The difference is between being a person of wisdom and knowledge (adding long-term value), or being a person of avarice and greed (engaging only in the short-term pursuit of money). One of my long-held mantras is, "If you don't add value to your customers, someone else will."

Single-tenant restaurant real estate finance fit my return formula. I believed we could get a higher rate of return for our investors than the risk we were undertaking, and simultaneously add value to our franchisee customers whose margins were wide enough so they could afford our lease rental rates, and who needed capital to grow their operations.

The Assets of My Mental Balance Sheet Pay Off!

The long years I spent building the assets of My Mental Balance Sheet had prepared me to understand the basics of the following, ***all of which I needed to know to be able to lead this venture:***

a. Commercial finance;

b. Marketing, communication, and sales;

c. How to work with investment banks on Wall Street: how to raise funds, how commercial banking worked, and how to successfully borrow funds;

d. How to work with the government and how to obtain insurance guarantees;

e. How to evaluate risk, both quantitative and emotional; and

f. How to build a management team for my company with the distinctive skills necessary to create and manage a successful organization.

I was grateful that the assets I had added over the years to my Mental Balance Sheet enabled me to take action **when the right opportunity arose.** It was apparent to me that "single-tenant" real estate was it.

In 1980, when we started FFCA, the Federal Reserve was trying to substantially reduce inflation. In an effort to do so, they raised interest rates. The theory was that raising interest rates would slow economic growth and therefore slow inflation. They were successful. The prime rate (which is a short-term bank borrowing rate for high quality companies) fluctuated that year from 12% to 21.5%, much of the year at the higher rate, and the 10-year United States treasury rate was 12%. Both rates have come down substantially since that time, and at the time of this writing, the 10-year treasury rate is very low, at just 2.85%.

In the meantime, FFCA was offering to retail investors an opportunity to invest in a whole new class of assets, single-tenant restaurant real estate, which many investors had previously considered to be risky investments. Once fully invested, we predicted a cash yield to the investors of 9%. Approximately 40% of that amount was sheltered from taxes by depreciation taken on the buildings and equipment. On a pre-tax basis, depending on the investors' tax bracket, this would convert to a 12-14% gross annual pre-tax return for investors. U.S. Treasury obligations, depending on their duration were yielding from 12%-20%. In other words, the best credit in the world was yielding to investors a substantially higher return on investment, and that was stiff competition. However, we prevailed and were able to raise money because intelligent retail investors knew interest rates would come down (and together with the interest rates, the yield on the United States Treasury obligations would be lower), so our 9% cash plus depreciation shelter, over the long term, was appealing.

We raised $22 million in 1980 in our first partnership with Hardee's Lease Partners. It took us an entire year to put this first venture together. It was difficult, but we persisted. The money was to be invested in real estate and equipment owned by the partnerships and leased to Hardee's franchisees. Our retail investors were long-term thinkers. They could see that fast food restaurant chains were rapidly growing and thought that it would be a good long-term investment, and they were right.

Our customers, the franchisees of Hardee's restaurants, were growing rapidly and needed capital for restaurant real estate and equipment. In order to acquire more franchisee-customers, I "took a page" from my economic courses in college and proposed that we provide financing like "merchant bankers"*: we would provide 100% financing for the building, land, and equipment for qualified franchisees. We would own the assets debt-free (to further mitigate our risk) and then lease them all back to the franchisees. The franchisees would only have to make lease payments, and would not have the burden of debt amortization (payback of loans). Consequently, their cash flow and return on their invested capital would be higher.

I believed that operating like a merchant banker would entice the franchisees to have a greater interest in the financing we could provide, as opposed to what they could obtain from commercial banks. In reality, our 100% financing offer compared very favorably to traditional bank financing which (when available), generally only offered up to 75% debt financing. In many instances, the franchisee had to put up 25% of the cost of the real estate and equipment. The need to devote that capital to their real estate and equipment meant the franchisee had less money to dedicate to growth. Of course, this made it more difficult for them to expand their operations. In most cases, the franchisees didn't even have the 25% equity requirement. Many times traditional bankers are so risk-averse that they advance (loan) just enough money for their customers to go broke. My "merchant banking" approach and 100% financing offer allowed the franchisees to prosper and to grow their businesses.

We were **adding value** to both the investors and to our customers, the franchisees, and so our company was profitable and grew. My past experiences (empiricism) and Mental Balance Sheet helped me to determine how we would operate the new company, Franchise Finance Corporation of America.

The company structure of FFCA fit our moral compass and risk tolerance level as **value was added over the long-term for all participants**. Every good financial entrepreneur wants to make sure that the rate of return they can make is higher than the risk they are taking. Because there is always going to be error, there has to be margin for error. Our margins (ratio of income to costs) were wide, allowing for error and/or unforeseen events, which **always seem to occur**. We believed that as long as we were disciplined and stuck to our "bottom-up credit" financial formula, while simultaneously only doing business with qualified franchisees and well-known brands, we had an opportunity to grow and put more restaurant real estate assets under our management.

This growth opportunity became a reality, as is evident from the following list of limited partnership offerings that we completed in the 1980s and the total amount raised:

1. Hardee's Lease Partners – 1980 - $25 million
2. Arby's Lease Partners – 1981 - $20 million
3. Insured Income Properties – 1982 - $30 million
4. Insured Income Properties – 1983 - $50 million
5. Insured Pension Investors – 1983 - $30 million
6. Insured Income Properties – 1984 - $100 million
7. Insured Pension Investors – 1984 - $50 million
8. Insured Income Properties – 1985 - $100 million
9. Insured Income Investors – 1985 - $100 million

10. Guaranteed Hotel Investors – 1985 - $100 million

11. Insured Income Properties – 1986 - $100 million

12. Participating Income Properties – 1986 - $75 million

13. Insured Income Properties – 1988 - $150 million

14. Scottsdale Land Trust Properties - $50 million

15. Participating Income Properties - $100 million

16. Fiduciary Capital Partners - $75 million

17. Participating Income Properties – 1988 - $100 million

TOTAL   **$1.23 Billion Equity**

You may have noticed in the list above that as the years passed the size of the assets managed by the limited partnerships increased substantially. As the list illustrates, in approximately 10 years, FFCA raised approximately $1.23 billion in equity!

From time to time it has been suggested to me that I was "lucky" in founding and helping to build FFCA and its related entities. I respectfully disagreed. **My definition of luck is when opportunity meets preparedness.** Thanks to the assets of my Mental Balance Sheet, which I had been building over the previous years, **I was prepared** when the opportunity presented itself and recognized it. **Every business venture I had pursued up until this point had provided valuable assets for my Mental Balance Sheet.** Without those assets, I would not have understood how to work with Wall

Street, how the guarantees functioned, how to create an investment vehicle that brokers at investment banks would be able to sell to investors, how to create a sales team that could talk to the stock brokers and assist in raising money and talking to the franchisees. In addition to all that, we also had to invest the money, collect the rent, manage the defaults, and service the leases. We had to build the infrastructure of FFCA as it grew relationships, contacts, computer systems, and management team. I had a working knowledge of all this that I had learned through the multiple business pursuits in which I had worked over the years. **My Mental Balance Sheet Assets provided me the knowledge that got me in the game.** This principle applies to any business that you may start or operate in your life: The size is really not material. Whether you own or operate a small business or a large business, you need to have the assets you gained from your past experiences to help you know how to start, manage and grow it. Thereafter you have to continually re-engineer your business and yourself to changing market conditions to remain successful.

In my view, there are three kinds of "players" in the business world: the investor, the risk-taker, and the gambler. Two of them will sometimes fail. The investor may fail because he assumes there will be no change in the world, but the world is always changing, and it sometimes moves right on past the investor as it changes. As an example, people thought General Motors would exist forever, but in

2008 the company would have gone broke without the intervention of the U.S. government. General Motors did not keep up with the changing world. The gambler will also fail, because the same forces that drive him to succeed will drive him to lose. My uncle was a gambler, and he died broke. I remember my Mother talking about it. That's why I'm not a gambler. I like to do things that make sense. Gambling doesn't make sense as I know the odds are against me. The casinos in Las Vegas weren't built to lose money. It is the knowledgeable risk-taker who will succeed, because he assumes constant change in the world. The knowledgeable risk-taker is like the missile that is constantly adjusting its rudder as it reassesses its environment and flies to the target. Our world is constantly changing, and you need to be prepared for that. It is changing even more rapidly now than it was when I first started out in the business world. Your success is more likely once you understand and adopt this principle.

As I had hoped and anticipated, the opportunity for growth in the FFCA venture was tremendous. At the end of the 1980s, the partnerships under FFCA management owned (with no debt) over 1,000 properties across the U.S. The partnerships also collectively had 170,000 retail investors and were sending out combined cash distributions of nearly $120,000,000 annually. We had a substantial business! This financial result was obtained with an initial equity investment of $100,000 and a $250,000 bank line of credit! We started with a small partnership with Hardee's, and we learned how to manage, grow and run the operations of a large business that grew to 250 employees.

Building the Staff of a Business Enterprise

An important point I want to make with regard to building the staff of a business enterprise: always hire employees and vendors, where possible, who are looking for an "exciting journey" and who want to be part of something bigger than themselves. People work for money, but I've learned that more importantly, once they have sustenance and have their basic needs fulfilled people who are of good values and high character wants to be part of something important. They want to feel like their lives have some meaning. They themselves may not be capable of creating that something, but they can recognize it. They want to be a part of a growing company and work with people whose values are similar to theirs. They're willing to be uncomfortable, and willing to take responsibility if you give it to them, because when they achieve something, then they realize the joy of achievement. **Give them responsibility and then make them be responsible.**

It is also crucial to surround yourself with people of high character, who share your moral compass, your risk tolerance, who are highly motivated and have a powerful work ethic. I'm fortunate in that I've had the privilege of working with a small group of people who have been associates of mine for 15-30 plus years. They all have different jobs and different skill sets than I have. But they all have the same values, the same risk tolerance, are of high moral character, and we built these companies together. And we're still together. Leadership in these companies comes from the top down. The values of the leaders and the way they think will permeate the entire organization. People who think like you do will stay, and people who have different value systems will leave. We strongly reinforce our value systems in all of our companies, and that is a crucial asset and element of the success of each of those companies.

In 1979 the basic assets of my Mental Balance Sheet were in place and I had found the business opportunity I had been looking for. I had added assets to my Mental Balance Sheet with every business opportunity I pursued, but all through the years **I had stayed focused on my ultimate goal**. I didn't allow myself to be **distracted by minutiae**. All of the pieces began to fit into place. The whole FFCA enterprise was very entrepreneurial, because we had to put so many disparate pieces together. It was like putting "square pegs" into "round holes." The franchisees didn't really understand how sales-leaseback worked. At first, the market didn't really understand the investment product, either. So our salespeople had to be very good communicators. As I trained our staff, I used a lot of the Mental Balance Sheet assets I had gained from working with Charlie Sharpe in the life insurance business about how to be a good communicator. We had to sell to the stock brokers, to the investors who would be investing capital, and to the franchisees who would be using the capital. In the early stages, these endeavors were complicated to execute and continue to be so to this day.

Adapting to Changing Economic Environments

After we had successfully put together all of the pieces of the enterprise, the next challenge was the initial execution of our business model and adapting it to changing economic environments, which we have done for the past 39 years and continue to do (2019) through S|T|O|R|E| Capital Corporation, our current company, which is listed on the New York Stock Exchange under the ticker symbol "STOR". In the mid-1980s, we encountered our first big challenge due to the changing economic environment: the fast food industry had started to mature, and it was no longer feasible to put a fast food restaurant on every street corner with a high likelihood of success. We had too many seats in restaurants without enough customers to fill them. The industry began to consolidate, as margins shrank and small operators began to fail. Over and over again, we witnessed franchisees that grew to operate 5-10 restaurants, were then distracted by running a construction company or by some other unrelated activities, and would go broke. The public investment partnerships that we managed didn't have any debt, therefore in the event of default by an operator, we avoided any lender discussions. We could foreclose and take back the restaurant and then lease it to a new operator or just outright sell the property. The end result was that we ended up with a whole "stable" of really good operators, people who could run a restaurant well. We had one Arby's operator who ran approximately 1,000 stores.

Adapting to the Changing World

In the mid-1980s when the consolidation of the fast food industry began, we had to decide whether we were going to remain the entrepreneurial shop that I had created, or become a fully-integrated finance company. We opted to create a finance company and I knew I needed to have professional managers working with me. When you employ experienced, intelligent, highly motivated people of high character, you don't have to tell them every step that they have to take. And to repeat, the key is to **give them responsibility and make them be responsible.** As you will see, our team was able to efficiently deal with the difficulties of a changing economic economy.

In the late 1980s, we hit a roadblock when E. F. Hutton, our capital source, got into legal and financial difficulties and was forced to merge with Lehman Brothers. This was a shocking development. E. F. Hutton had once been one of the largest investment banking houses on Wall Street, but due to the incorrect vision of some of its senior management, the whole firm almost collapsed. Once again, it was brought home to me in a painful way that **the world is constantly changing.** I couldn't believe that this huge investment banking firm—one of the largest firms on Wall Street—had essentially failed! And it had failed almost overnight. Our source of capital was gone and we had to adapt to that. We had to figure out how we could continue to operate and grow our business. We had to cut our staff by 50-60%, which was really hard, but we didn't have any choice. The economist, Joseph Schumpeter, whose ideas I studied in college, taught me the economic principle that "capitalism is creative destruction." This means that capitalism requires companies to constantly adapt and re-adapt with new more efficient models to meet current needs, which is what we had to do if we wanted to survive.

After making such significant cuts in our staff, our income from fees exceeded our expenses and we could survive without adding new assets under management. We were **long-term thinkers** and had set up our company so that the assets we had under management would provide continuing income without adding any new assets under management. This allowed us to stay in business and survive during adverse times.

After much research, we decided that the best option was to merge ("roll up") the fast food partnerships under our management and create a Real Estate Investment Trust (REIT). A REIT is an investment vehicle for real estate that is comparable to a mutual fund, allowing both small and large investors to acquire ownership in real estate ventures, to own (and in some cases operate) single-tenant real estate, commercial properties such as apartment complexes, hospitals, office buildings, timberland, warehouses, hotels and shopping malls.[1] The U.S. Congress passed laws allowing the formation of REITs to provide small investors the opportunity to invest in real estate like the large, tax-exempt investors in the United States, such as the California Public Employees' Retirement System (CalPERS). Today investors of all types and sizes invest in REITs.

Out of the 17 partnerships under FFCA management, 11 were invested in restaurant real estate. After many regulatory issues, the merger of FFCA and its management and restaurant partnership company was reconfigured as a REIT and was completed in 1994. Thereafter, the new FFCA (the REIT) began trading on the New York Stock Exchange (NYSE). It had one billion dollars of equity and no debt, while owning approximately 1,000 single-tenant properties.

Standing My Ground

This process was called a "roll-up," and ours was the largest roll-up or partnership merger at that time that had ever been done and the first of its kind. I had millions of my own money invested to complete this transaction. Then along came the State of California. They didn't like roll-ups and weren't going to approve ours because investors had lost their money in some of the roll-ups that had been done in California. The California regulators told us that they were going to make their blue sky laws "extra-territorial" (*i.e.,* effective across the United States). "Blue Sky" laws are state regulations designed to protect investors against securities fraud by requiring the sellers of new issues of securities that aren't listed on organized stock exchanges to register those securities and provide financial details. A state with "Blue Sky" laws may prohibit the sale of any security in its State for purely discretionary or bureaucratic reasons. The hoped-for result is that investors will be able to base their judgments on trustworthy data.[2] I had never heard of a State trying to apply its laws extra-territorially, and we would have been "up a creek without a paddle" if we had let California proceed as they were threatening to, nor did I believe that they had the right to do so. We had been working on this merger for a year and a half and we were very frustrated by the State of California's position. We decided to hire Willie Barnes, a lawyer in private practice in California who was the former Securities Commissioner of the State of California. I asked for his advice and he said that we had a very good case and might consider suing the State of California, although he said that none of his other clients had done that as they were all "afraid" of the State. But I knew that **we were right**, and California was dead wrong, so we had no choice but to negotiate with them, and if necessary, resort to litigation.

At this point in my story, I want to take a moment to talk about working with lawyers. There will be times, such as when you're working in an area with complicated laws and regulations, when you will need the advice of good lawyers. The crucial point is that although you should listen to your lawyers, ultimately, you (the businessperson) should make the business decisions and lead them. Attorneys are trained to look back at case law and legal precedents (what has already been decided by the courts); they are not generally risk-takers, as opposed to entrepreneurs and business people, who, unlike attorneys, look forward to determine opportunity. Attorneys often make the mistake of thinking they have good business judgment because so many of their clients don't lead them, and they *ask the lawyers* for business advice and what they should do. Lawyers should never be making the business decisions. My view is that lawyers should give legal advice (and if asked, business advice) to their clients to help them ensure they comply with any applicable laws and regulations, but ultimately, the business decisions should be made by the entrepreneur or businessperson.

Returning to the problem in California, our attorney, Willie Barnes, arranged a meeting for us with the California State securities regulators. Willie, some FFCA staff and I walked into a room containing a long conference table that was lined with the bureaucrats who worked for the California Securities Commission. At first, we had a nice "visit" with everybody. We all smiled at one another and chatted, but there was no indication that California was going to change their position. The energy of the situation completely changed when Willie Barnes suddenly looked over everyone in the room and announced, "I want you people to know that my client will do whatever they have to do to get this transaction completed, because your position is wrong. My client believes this is a fair, just and equitable transaction for all of his investors. Let me repeat: we will do whatever we have to do to make sure this transaction is completed!" He stood up and turned to walk out, beckoning to me, "Come on, Mort!" and as I walked out with him (together with our staff), I thought, *There goes my millions invested right down the tube.* But once we were out of that room, Willie reassured me, "We got 'em, Mort!" And once again, our strategy worked. **Because we knew our opposition, and we knew we were in the right.** A few days later, the State regulators called Willie and told him that if we'd do "one small thing" and make minor changes in the terms of the offering, they'd approve the transaction for clearance in California and would not try to interfere with our clearances around the rest of the country. So I told Willie that I'd agree to do what they wanted us to do. The roll-up took two years and we merged all of our 11 restaurant partnerships together into the FFCA REIT, a new New York Stock Exchange listed company.

The World Changed, and the Competition Increased

During the years that our partnerships existed (in the 1980s), they were "below the radar screen" (the visibility) of the major financial institutions in the U.S. such as large banks and finance companies. When we merged our partnerships into the REIT and we were publicly traded (so we had to file quarterly and annual reports with the S.E.C.), we quickly became aware that these institutions could not only see what we were doing, they could also figure out our profit margins and related risks, and recognize that we were able to meet our earnings projections on a quarterly calendar by purchasing and servicing single-tenant real estate assets with long-term 15-20 year leases. It did not escape them that we were meeting our financial goals and making a larger return for our investors than the risks we undertook, and simultaneously, our franchisee customers, the users of our capital, were prospering. We were defining and expanding the market for single-tenant real estate assets that were essential to operations. Inefficient financial markets (industries) that are discovered by forward-looking entrepreneurs (such as we are) are "fair game" for large, well-capitalized financial institutions. When it becomes clear that the risks being taken are reasonable, these larger institutions will get into the market, and they can drive you right out of that market because it is difficult to compete with their ability to obtain significantly less-expensive capital using their large balance sheets.

After our activities got the attention of the larger institutions (due to our quarterly and annual filings with the S.E.C.), many of the large banks and finance companies called on us. It soon became apparent to us that their cost of capital was substantially lower than ours. They were much larger than we were, and if they decided to compete with us, they could easily do so, possibly driving us out of the market. As a result, in 2001 we agreed to sell FFCA to G. E. Capital for $2.1 billion in cash and debt assumption, which included a combined investment and servicing portfolio, which had increased from 1,000 properties in 1984 to more than 6,200 properties in the U.S. and Canada in 2001. We sold FFCA to G. E. Capital because we realized that we would continue to have a lot of difficulty competing with them and others due to their lower capital cost.

We had progressed from the early-to-mid 1980s when we were an entrepreneurial organization, to becoming more of a fully-integrated real estate finance company. During the mid-1980s, I realized I needed help. **I needed people who had skill sets that I didn't have.** That was when I met Chris Volk, who eventually became the President and Chief Operating Officer of FFCA and the President/CEO of Spirit Finance and S|T|O|R|E Capital. Chris was a banker who I first met in Atlanta, Georgia. He was doing interim or construction financing for FFCA at a Georgia Bank. I needed interim financing (loans to build a restaurant property) for our franchisee customers, which would be guaranteed by an FFCA-managed partnership and paid off when the restaurant was completed and occupied. I had difficulty finding a bank that would do this. Chris took on handling the interim financing in the South and eventually all over the U.S. Chris is a brilliant financier and professional manager. I knew he had the skills we needed to continue moving FFCA forward.

One of the great innovations that Chris suggested (of many) was an adjustment to our "bottom-up credit" model: in addition to limiting the funds we advanced to the replacement cost of the franchisees' buildings and equipment, Chris proposed that we add to the model the concept of unit level cash flow coverage (which I included in our earlier discussion of our credit model), so we could easily see how well each unit was performing. As previously mentioned, the theory was that 20% of the units might produce 80% of the cash flow and we should look at each unit as an individual "profit center." He also suggested we require our franchisee customers to send us their unit level financial statements every quarter. If we see from the financial statements that the customer's cash flow is going down, we call him before he tells us he can't make his lease payments, ask what's wrong, and make suggestions to try to help him improve his operations. Our goal is to determine if the customer is part of the solution or part of the problem. It's a service we provide to our customers. Our database provides us with significant industry information. We call this approach "proactive intervention" and it is very effective. This is a significant **value added** to our relationship with our customers.

As time went on, the senior staff and I began to understand that the most successful people have two primary characteristics: **intellect and instinct**. Intellect can be improved and perfected from "book learning" part of the intellectual capital of your Mental Balance Sheet. It's the application of knowledge about your field of endeavor. Instinct is a rare commodity. It's the working of your subconscious mind that tells you when somebody is misrepresenting or when something isn't going to work because it doesn't "feel right." I believe your subconscious mind to a large extent (based on empiricism) provides the basis of your instinct, which will tell you when something isn't going to work, even if it looks like it will work from an intellectual viewpoint. The incredibly important skill is learning to trust both your intellect and your instinct, and **getting them to work together**. We have found them both to be very important for credit analysis in all of our companies. Remember the early discussion in this book about servo-mechanisms from *Psycho Cybernetics* and my guided missile military training which was an analogy for the training of your subconscious mind and goal seeking. These techniques should be of assistance to you in ANY LEVEL OF ENDEAVOR and/or in your personal life that you decide to accomplish.

Keeping Our Team Together

By late 2002, all of the senior staff at FFCA had departed the GE Capital Unit which had acquired FFCA. The entrepreneurial management style of our team did not fit well at GE, which like many large companies, had a more bureaucratic style of management driven, amongst other things, by their large balance sheet and top-heavy management style.

I have worked with some of the members of our management team for over 30 years. Although we each had different skill sets, we shared the same values, moral character, risk tolerance, and powerful work ethic. We all benefitted from working together. We realized there were still large numbers of small-to-medium businesses with single-tenant operationally essential real estate that needed financing, and that we could fill some of that need. Therefore, our management team decided to start a new company in 2003. We called it "Spirit Finance," which was inspired by the Spirit statue. The statue had been on the FFCA grounds, and when GE bought FFCA, they gave us the statue, which I took to our ranch in Arizona and set it up in a prominent location. The people at GE told me, "This statue represents you, Mort—not us—and you should have it." I was grateful to take it! Subsequently, my wife Donna and I donated the statue to Arizona State University and it is now in front of the W. P. Carey Business School, a very appropriate place for it to be, and where we believe it is inspiring students.

Spirit Finance's mission was the same as that of FFCA: to finance single-tenant operationally essential real estate. We managed Spirit Finance from 2003 until late 2009 when, in our never-ending search for lower cost of capital, Spirit Finance was sold to a consortium led by Macquarie Bank, LLC, an Australian investment banking firm, for $3.5 billion. They had earned a reputation for securing low-cost capital across the world. At the time of the sale, Spirit's core markets for investment and our definition of single-tenant operationally essential real estate had been expanded beyond restaurants to include free-standing automotive dealers, parts and service facilities, drug stores, educational facilities, movie theaters, supermarkets and other retail, distribution and service businesses. **We had refined and broadened the definition of single-tenant real estate to include real estate locations, from which a company operates its business and generates sales and profits, which makes the location a profit center, and therefore, fundamentally an integral part of that business.**

I often ask our staff to answer the question, "Does man make history, or does history make man?" I believe the answer is both. The following is a good example: we started Spirit Finance and managed its growth very well. The "Great Recession" of 2008 came shortly after the Macquarie sale and with it Macquarie lost its ability to raise low cost capital funds. Consequently, the recession (which was beyond our control) changed our management team's direction. In the beginning we made history by starting Spirit Finance, however the Great Recession in 2008 removed our source of new capital, which is essential for a REIT to grow. History and outside events beyond our control affected us and caused us to change direction.

After much acrimony and assaults on our moral compass, our management team severed relations with Spirit Finance. Unfortunately, our disagreements resulted in expensive litigation, which lasted for 18 months until it was finally settled. My view of litigation is to avoid it whenever possible; however, if you believe you have tried all other available remedies, litigation is an alternative in our country that allows each of us to seek justice from another party for our grievance. My experience has been that our justice system (which I have utilized on a limited basis) works pretty well. You should make sure you have good lawyers, deep pockets and the courage to deal with harsh tactics that the legal profession sometimes employs. We believed that our positions were correct in the few lawsuits in which we have been involved, and the results proved we were right as we prevailed. Our justice system is available to all of us. You should not hesitate to use it when you need it. However, use it only as a last resort because of its high cost and time delays.

After the Great Recession of 2008, the U.S. Congress passed the "Dodd-Frank Wall Street Reform and Consumer Protection Act of

2010," and the Basel Accords were issued by the Basel Committee on Banking Supervision. The results of these new laws were the increased regulation and capital requirements of financial institutions—regulations that made commercial banks even less responsive to the long-term capital needs of the middle-market companies that we at S|T|O|R|E Capital target. This meant more opportunity for S|T|O|R|E Capital and clearly illuminated the need for our management teams to "stay the course," because the new environment opened up opportunities that we had not previously seen.

S|T|O|R|E Capital was founded in May 2011, largely through the efforts of Chris Volk, STORE's President and CEO, and with backing from large institutional investors. "STORE" is an acronym for single-tenant operational real estate. Our management team grew and incubated the company through to the pricing of its initial public offering in November of 2014, and it is currently listed and trades on the New York Stock Exchange (NYSE). Its symbol is "STOR".

We formed S|T|O|R|E Capital to take advantage of the market opportunity that we had already been addressing in prior companies but which was enlarged by the passage of the Dodd-Frank Act. Banks had less interest in addressing the long-term capital needs of middle-market and larger, non-rated companies. S|T|O|R|E now had an opportunity to offer them a superior alternative to financing their profit-center real estate with traditional mortgage or bank debt and their own equity using our sale- leaseback financing.

It was exhilarating as *finally*, institutional investors recognized our 30-plus-year track record, embraced our "bottom-up credit" model and provided initial backing. The current financial environment is the best we have ever seen for the execution of our model. The market is large—we estimate it is currently in excess of $2.5 trillion. The lease and available debt rates are attractive. Our customers, both capital investors and users of capital, benefit from our financing as long-term value is made available for both.

We have been in this business since 1980 (39 years at the time of this writing). When we started, long-term government bonds yielded from 12% to approximately 16%. They currently yield only 2.85%. We have successfully managed these businesses using the early "bottom-up credit" formula we entrepreneurially invented, while operating through a variety of economic environments. All of the single-tenant real estate partnerships our team managed has either equaled or exceeded our original projections. We've added nuances to our original model, while always adding value to our investors and customers, the providers and users of capital. Our investors run the gamut from retail to institutional investors, and we are one of the leaders in creating a new class of real estate: "SINGLE-TENANT OPERATIONALLY ESSENTIAL" real estate, which has allowed me to reach my goal of being a part of a team that built substantial companies and added value to our system.

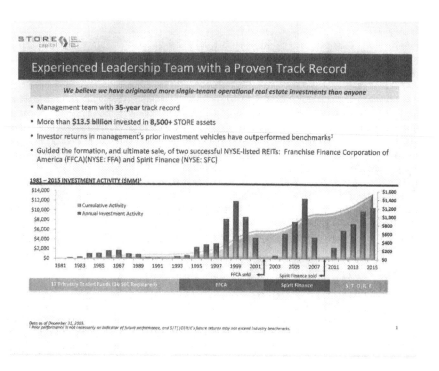

As you have seen while reading this book, I engaged in many different business endeavors over the course of my career. As I participated in those various ventures, I always kept my ultimate goal in sight. As I gained assets for my Mental Balance Sheet from each business I worked in, I was also refining my ultimate goal. Over the years, whenever I saw that what I was doing couldn't quite reach my goal, I would leave that pursuit and move on to the next venture, looking to find the right opportunity. Finally, I encountered the need for single-tenant real estate finance. That was, and continues to be, the most successful and greatest adventure of my career, and it required constant personal growth.

The assets of my Mental Balance Sheet are what made it possible for me to assist in creating the bottom-up credit model, sell it to Wall Street firms and fast food restaurant franchisees, and build the businesses I started. The assets of my Mental Balance Sheet enabled me to form and lead extremely capable management teams to make it all happen. The wisdom that I acquired from my philosophy studies in college, from my early cultural background and business experiences helped me decide when it was time to step aside and let other members of our management team such as Chris Volk, STORE's President/Chief Executive Officer (CEO), lead the company. Over time, we became less entrepreneurial and needed to be more professionally managed, which aligns with his skill sets and those of other members of our management team.

The following are a few of the many people who contributed to our success and who I believe were and continue to be indispensable in operating our businesses over the years:

Chris Volk, is an extraordinarily capable finance professional, banker, and manager. He joined FFCA in the mid-1980s and is vital in all aspects of our business. He became Chief Operating Officer (COO) of FFCA and CEO of Spirit Finance. Today he is CEO of S|T|O|R|E Capital and has led the way towards producing returns that attract institutional investors, while establishing systems and professional management that make S|T|O|R|E Capital "best in class" for purveyors of net lease real estate capital.

Paul Belitz, our lead lawyer since 1980, has steered us through the legal complexities of all our companies and assists us in managing our other lawyers, neither of which are easy tasks. Paul was the first in his family to go to college (and then to law school) and had to learn for himself many of the lessons of this book. He has also contributed many hours without charge to the Fleischer Scholars Program over the last several years.

Cathy Long, S|T|O|R|E Capital's Chief Financial Officer (CFO), has worked with me in all our companies since 1980 when she was a CPA at Arthur Anderson. Over the years, she has grown into an extremely capable CFO. I call her the "Iron Lady" (after Margaret Thatcher, former Prime Minster of England) as I never worry about our financial activities when Cathy is in charge.

Mary Fedewa is the COO of S|T|O|R|E Capital. We have been working together since 2001. Her vision, energy and professional management skills are responsible for a large part of S|T|O|R|E Capital's success.

Enjoying life and the benefits of our labors is a byproduct of our work. I believe that **this country**, since its founding, and despite its problems (which it has always had), still **provides the most fertile ground for individual achievement**. Re-read Chapter One of this book. You live in America and its framework makes everything possible. **The ultimate reward of building your Mental Balance Sheet is to accomplish and live your vision/dream.** America affords you that opportunity.

Some of the personal visions and dreams that my wife Donna and I have been able to accomplish and enjoy because of the success of our companies are as follows:

- The Fleischer Museum, which was our cultural contribution to the Scottsdale community. It existed from 1988 until 2001. In the late 1980s, we were the financing partner with a developer, Westcorp and together built an office park in Scottsdale called "The Perimeter Center." We raised $50 million with E.F. Hutton and were able to build the Perimeter Center, which included a building for FFCA. We have a collection of American Impressionism California School paintings that we began purchasing in the early 1980s. I was interviewed by the Mayor of Scottsdale and said something about creating a museum. There was a reporter in attendance, and the next day the Scottsdale paper announced, "Fleischer Museum Comes to

Scottsdale." I said to my wife Donna, "This is a great idea! Let's do it—and you are the new director." Donna is a horticulturist, is very artistic, and loves beauty, so she was the natural choice for this position. She took it very seriously and did a great job. For 15 years, the Fleischer Museum was open in the lobby of the FFCA office building at no charge to the public. It was our cultural contribution to the community and was closed shortly after FFCA was sold to GE Capital.

- We established the Fleischer Foundation. Its primary mission is to sponsor entrepreneurship and business-related activities such as the Fleischer Scholars Program.

- MorDo Ranch and Horse Thief Basin Ranch:
  Donna and I love the west. In 1990, we bought some land and built a ranch in North Scottsdale where for years we raised quarter horses and Donna showed them. Fifteen years ago, we bought Horse Thief Basin Ranch, a cattle ranch in Montana where we raise Black Angus cattle.

- Western Memorabilia:
  In the early 1980s, I started collecting Western Memorabilia, such as saddles, chaps, Colt six-shooters, Winchesters, holsters, and spurs. I have enjoyed this hobby immensely.

The success of our companies has allowed us the opportunity to fill our lives with exciting adventures. The Fleischer Museum and impressionist paintings introduced us to a new world and we met people who substantially broadened our horizons. The Western collection and ranches allowed us to live what we call a "Modern Western Lifestyle." MorDo Ranch is located near Scottsdale, Arizona with all the available amenities of a large city. Horse Thief Basin Ranch in Montana is a working cattle ranch with log homes and provides us the opportunity to unwind and live a more basic ranch life. Together they allow us to enjoy the lifestyle of the new and old west.

All of these hobbies have added immeasurably to the quality of our lives. America affords all of us the same kind of opportunities that my family has enjoyed. They are available to some degree at ALL LEVELS of accomplishment. It is up to you to choose to work toward your goals, visions, and accomplishments. Dreams CAN become reality.

Now that you've nearly completed this book and have read about my life's journey, take this opportunity to once again complete the blank Mental Balance Sheet, filling in the assets I gained and liabilities I acquired based on what you have read thus far about my life and my experiences with the single-tenant real estate finance business.

Next, compare the assets and liabilities you wrote in the blank Mental Balance Sheet with the assets and liabilities I noted myself on my Mental Balance Sheet (following) after my experiences with the single-tenant real estate finance business.

MR. FLEISCHER'S MENTAL BALANCE SHEET
(1949-present) Single-Tenant Real Estate Finance

ASSETS
_____

Empirical Knowledge

- Loving and supportive parents
- "Huck Finn" type environment:
    - Hunting-fishing-swimming in creeks
- Ran my first business (lawn mowing)
    - Introduction to use of leverage to increase profits
- First Job-Janitor at Woolworth
    - Beginning to understand my addiction to the joy of achievement
- Learned basic leadership principles
- The art of negotiation—understand your opponents—the art of bluffing
- Benefits of taking initiative
    - All opportunities have critical deal making moments (airport meeting)
- Give people responsibility and make them responsible
- The importance of focusing on and developing goals while ignoring minutiae
- The value of and how to use marketing and advertising
- The need to develop and encourage teamwork
- How to develop, train and motivate a sales force
- The difference between intellect and instinct and knowing how to command both
- Intellectual resources and assets make the difference between success and failure
- The art of becoming a direct salesman and applying those skills toward being a better communicator

- The importance of customer service—if you don't add value and serve the customer, someone else will
- The "take away" strategy I learned in the life insurance business works in many other circumstances
- How life insurance companies work and are financed
- How life insurance companies can earn money on their liabilities
- How actuaries work – utilizing statistics and probability
- The art of turning an option on a company into a substantial profit (life insurance company)
- The American judicial system is not perfect, but generally works
  - the importance of complying with applicable laws and regulations
- Use attorneys for legal advice, not business judgments
  - You may need attorneys that are specialist in certain legal fields
- Capital markets (non-bank) are broad and deep in America
- Business cycles are inevitable as they are part of our capitalistic system
- Coal mining is management, capital, regulatory maintenance and labor (unions) intensive
  - Coal is a commodity and subject to price fluctuation. The risks are difficult to quantify
- I defined the difference between quantitative risks (projections) and emotional risks (sleep at night)
  - You need to understand your level of risk tolerance
- The value of U.S. government guarantees and licenses (SBA and radio stations)
- Learned when to exit (sell) a business (coal mine, FFCA, Spirit)
- Any business, large or small, can fail when it has strong competition, improper vision or leadership (E.F. Hutton)
- A combination of entrepreneurial and professional management skills are necessary to run most businesses

- In all of business there in one constant – CHANGE
- It is important to differentiate between reality and perception in the world of finance (Insured Income Properties)
- Developed new credit model for inefficient growing single-tenant real estate – "bottom-up credit"
- Providing merchant banking type 100% financing made FFCA competitive with commercial banks
- Our team created "bottom-up credit" which allowed me to reach my lifetime business goals of building substantial companies by servicing a large inefficient market need "Single-Tenant Real Estate" which we estimate today to be approximately $2 trillion and is currently being addressed by the company I am Chairman of the Board of, "S|T|O|R|E Capital."

Intellectual Capital
- Public school education
- College education – Amongst other subjects, I studied:
    - Philosophy
    - Economics
    - Business courses
    - English
    - History
    - Geology
- I went to college to learn:
    - How to learn
    - How to write
    - How to think
    - How to be adaptable and get out of my comfort zone
- Eventually how to become an "Adaptive Master Learner"
- Eventually discovered and began using my brain (servo-mechanism)

as a goal seeking guidance system (*Psycho Cybernetics*) and also analogized it to a missile guidance system (military) in defining and seeking my goals

Moral Compass
- Traditional Judeo-Christian values
- Strong American mid-western values
- Stay true to the courage of my convictions and stay true to my value system
- Understood the value of respect, courage, character and individual motivation
- Develop and/or represent products that add value to the customer (no on vacant land—yes on single-tenant real estate finance)
- When disputes occur and you believe you are right, defend your position, even if the other side is a large entity (State of California)
- Do not do business with persons of suspicious, low moral character. It's not possible to make a good deal with a bad person

Liabilities

- I realized that I would permanently be in the position of **not knowing what I don't know**
- My inclination (entrepreneurial itch) to become involved in business I know very little about is risky
- My propensity for "Fire, Ready, Aim" when considering an opportunity has worked for me, but is more problematic in our current, more complex business environments. Remember the "instinct and intellect" discussion. Learn to use both with balance

In closing, for my Fleischer Scholars:
- I have no tolerance for gifted and talented persons who do not use hard work to improve themselves, their family, and society as a whole

CHAPTER NOTES

*In the days following the discovery of the New World, wealthy merchant bankers in Europe would approach a sea captain with a good reputation and offer to finance 100% a voyage to the New World. If the sea captain returned with furs, beads, tobacco (or whatever they could), the merchant bankers sold those items and gave the sea captain a healthy share of the profits.

[1]*Investopedia.* "Definition of a Real Estate Investment Trust." http://www.investopedia.com/terms/r/REIT.asp#ixzz3yguzsuct. Accessed January 28, 2016.

[2]*Investopedia.* "Definition of Blue Sky Laws." http://www.investopedia.com/terms/b/blueskylaws.asp#ixzz3ymDdZMUo. Accessed January 29, 2016.

CHAPTER TWELVE - NEVER GIVE UP!

As you've read about the various business endeavors I pursued, you may have noticed that I encountered obstacles, challenges and adversity in pretty much every one of them. It was at a fairly early point in my life—after both of my parents died when I was only 16—that I first encountered one of the harsh realities of life: if you want to succeed, you have to have a goal, fight for that goal, and keep fighting for it. You can never give up, no matter how tough "the going gets!" Losing both of my parents so young, moving in with relatives in a foreign (city) environment that was often hostile, transferring to a new high school where I was called a "yokel" and laughed at was a hard initiation into the world and could have "done me in," if I had given up. But I always believed that I could accomplish something of substance in my life.

I knew intuitively that I needed to go to college to acquire a world view and to experience more than the limited environment to which I had been exposed during my sheltered (albeit idyllic) childhood in rural Litchfield, Illinois. I gained a great education and added many valuable assets to my Mental Balance Sheet while at Washington University. My college experiences helped me to overcome my weaknesses. Although I didn't realize it at the time, my college studies also helped me to become a Master Adaptive Learner. I realized that the reasons a person should go to college are to learn:

1. **How to learn;**

2. **How to write;**

3. **How to solve problems;**

4. **How to think; and**

5. **How to be adaptable and continually get out of your comfort zone.**

Learning all of the foregoing skills and becoming a Master Adaptive Learner are valuable assets for *your* personal Mental Balance Sheet that will help you accomplish your long-term goals and will serve you for your entire lifetime. Attending college and becoming a Master Adaptive Learner is crucial to your success in business and life, because the world is constantly changing. If you are unable to adapt as the world changes, in our capitalistic system, you will be left behind. Capitalism is not a perfect system, but it is the best system in the world, and it is the system that has lifted mankind out of poverty. It is also Darwinian—think "survival of the fittest." As you operate your own business or another business in the future, you will need to be constantly changing as the world changes, and asking yourself, "How can I do what I'm doing, better? Is there anything that my competitor is doing better than I am doing it?" There may be times when your competitor *is* doing something better than you are, and when that is the case, you had better make adjustments, or watch your business decline.

As I began my business career, my ultimate long-term goal was not yet completely defined.   As I pursued my various business endeavors, I was establishing my goal. Whenever I saw that what I was doing didn't quite reach my goal, I would end that and move on to the next venture. I continued searching.   I didn't know for sure how or where I would find the complete realization of my goal, but I never stopped looking, I never stopped pressing forward, and I never stopped learning. From every business enterprise in which I engaged along the way, I gained many valuable assets for my Mental Balance Sheet, most of which helped me to achieve my final goal when I eventually completely defined it.

Finally, I encountered single-tenant real estate finance. That was, and continues to be, the most successful and greatest adventure of my career, and it required constant personal growth.

Just as it is a constant that the world is continually changing, it is also a constant that life is full of challenges, trials and adversity. You can either learn from those challenges, or you can "lie down" and let them run over you. Most of my life I have had to battle adversity as I pursued the accomplishment of my long-term goal. In my early post-college years, I even experienced a small amount of adversity from my family and friends, when they told me I was a "failure," that I "could never settle down," and that I "should have been a doctor, lawyer or a CPA."   To those well-intentioned, but misguided and uninformed, people, I guess I can say that my business accomplishments speak for themselves. As for my Pi Lambda Phi fraternity brothers at Washington University who nicknamed me "bumpkin," I have no hard feelings, especially as it is clear to me that I have "left all of them in the dust!

CHAPTER THIRTEEN – THE THREE-LEGGED STOOL

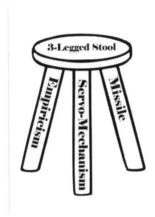

You may find a portion of this chapter redundant in that we are repeating the foreword, however I truly believe that the Three Legged Stool is **_THAT_** important to the process of building your mental balance sheet, becoming a Master Adaptive Learner, and consequently can be crucial to your successes in business and life. I clearly see that there were some PIVOTAL moments in my life that put in place the basic mental framework which I used in my journey. The first was when I discovered the philosophic school of *EMPIRICISM*—we are a sum of all our personal experiences. The second and third were when, during my military career, I learned how a *GUIDED MISSILE* seeks out a target and combined that process with what I learned from reading "*Psycho Cybernetics.*" I recognized my brain (when properly programmed) is a complicated *GOAL SEEKING SERVO-MECHANISM*. This knowledge provided the basic framework which I used in learning, establishing goals, and in business ventures. Combining them creates the **THREE LEGGED STOOL** that my career and personal life is based upon.

As I acquired knowledge (intellectual capital) and had more experiences (growth through empiricism) I was eventually able to manufacture new knowledge *i.e.*, be able to recognize opportunity (think single-tenant real estate), and develop new ways to take advantage of the opportunities I saw. UNDERSTANDING how to be a Master ADAPTIVE learner and continuing to build the assets of your Mental Balance Sheet in order to shape your own journey is a strategy that can last you a lifetime. I believe the world is full of good ideas. Executing them requires you to be relentless. As you will recall, I indicated earlier that the world resists change. I often say "When you have a good idea, you are 20% done and only have 80% left to go." That 80% is the EXECUTION of your idea.

I also triumphed over the challenges handed to me on more than one occasion by the "citizens" of Wall Street. As it turned out, the ultimate fulfillment of my long-term goal and achievement of great success began with the assistance of Wall Street (in the form of E. F. Hutton) because I never gave up trying to work with the public capital markets to achieve my dream.

Regardless, there were many "bumps" in the road along the way. I have mentioned that there were times when I would present an idea to an investment banker, who would smile, tell me "Great idea, Mort! We'd definitely like to get involved with that!" and then send me on my way, never again taking my phone calls, and stealing my ideas for his own profit. Whenever I was able to arrange a meeting with an investment banker, I never knew if I would leave the meeting with a new partner (who backed me) or a new competitor (who had stolen my idea). I did not let those short-term setbacks discourage me, however, because I continued pressing on in my desire to accomplish my ultimate goal and dream. Eventually, Wall Street actually did help make it come true. But in the early years, dealing with Wall Street was challenging.

There was one particular experience in New York early on, when I had no money. I was waiting for an appointment with someone at an investment banking firm who had agreed to listen to one of my ideas. It was a bitter cold day, in the middle of winter, and back then on Wall Street there were radiators in the buildings that were heated by steam. It was so cold that I put my feet up on the radiator to warm them while I waited for the opportunity to talk to the investment banker and hopefully sell one of my ideas to him. I've come a long way since then. But my point is, if I hadn't waited out in the cold on that winter day (and on subsequent days), if I had given up, I would now still be in the position I was in at that point in time.

I never let the fear of failure stop me. Failure is not to be feared, it is a part of learning. It is impossible to be successful without occasionally failing. The important thing is what you do with those failures. Do you learn from them, and add what you learned to your Mental Balance Sheet? Or do you let those failures defeat you and stop your progress?

In the 1960s when I was in the mergers and acquisitions business, I'd get an idea, and take it to Wall Street to try to sell it, but frequently, nobody would listen to me. I discovered early on that the people who would listen to me were the lower-level, smaller investment houses. I often was able to get appointments using the "take-it-away" strategy I had learned from the life insurance industry: I'd call a banker and tell them, "I've got a great idea, but I have a plane to catch as I have somebody else who's interested." The response was almost always, "Come right over!" In comparison, the big investment banks didn't generally listen much back when I was establishing my reputation in the industry. I kept fighting, kept trying, until people began to listen to me. But because I didn't give up, over time my ideas got better and the deals got better. Pretty soon, I had the attention of E. F. Hutton. When they liked my ideas, they'd invite me to lunch.

I remember one lunch meeting with E. F. Hutton when there was a platter of asparagus that appeared to be about two feet long. I didn't feel like I was getting anywhere in our meeting because the investment bankers kept giving me their "Wall Street run around." So I finally announced, "I'm not here for two foot-long asparagus. I came for money!" That got their attention and they started to listen.

I want to emphasize once more the importance of adding your moral compass to the assets of your Mental Balance Sheet. Your moral compass should be ever present in your mind. You should rely upon it for every decision you make, especially in regard to the people with whom you decide to associate and do business. Surround yourself with people of high character, and make sure that your close business associates and team share the same values. These characteristics will be of substantial assistance to you when faced with adversity. If your moral compass or your instincts warn you to stay away from someone, or to stay away from an endeavor, LISTEN and STAY AWAY! Surround yourself with people of high intelligence, who have skill sets you are lacking, and never forget that "**you don't know what you don't know**!"

Always be conscious of the limits of your risk tolerance. If an endeavor keeps you awake at night, worrying, then it exceeds your risk tolerance and is not a good fit for you. Be sure your business associates have a risk tolerance that is similar to yours.

Pursuing a career as an entrepreneur, businessman, or a professional manager of an existing business can be a wonderful, exciting and fulfilling life's journey. I believe money should be a byproduct of your work, not the ultimate goal. Making money is important, but once you can economically provide for yourself, I believe the journey becomes the most important. As you fulfill your life's pursuits as a businessman or entrepreneur, you are like an artist and the long-term ventures you create are your "canvas."

Add value to your investors and your customers and you will have profits. If you don't add value, somebody else will. Adding value to investors and customers should be a primary mission if a business is to succeed. If upon graduating from college you are working for a business of any size: small–medium–large, or if you start your own business, you won't survive unless you figure out what your competition is doing, and how you have to change your business to continue to meet the needs of the customer and your investors. If you don't add value to your customers over the long-term, you will have difficulty being successful in a capitalistic system.

We are goal-seeking creatures, and the joy of achievement is the life journey that long-term entrepreneurs crave. Use your personal experiences (EMPRICISM) and your brain (SERVO-MECHANISM). Remember *Psycho Cybernetics* and the missile heading to the target? I encourage you to enjoy the journey, and to always be mindful of the assets you are gaining for your personal Mental Balance Sheet. Always remember to stay focused on your goal! Do not be distracted by the minutiae of life that will surround you. Use the assets of your Mental Balance Sheet to assist you in knowing which parts of the minutiae you should discard. Define your goals carefully and readjust them to ever changing circumstances.

Be grateful that you are blessed to live in America. It is only in America that you can formulate and pursue your own dreams, your own long-term goals. When a company's stock is listed on the New York Stock Exchange, the senior staff of the company is invited to a luncheon, and the company Chairman and President both have an opportunity to speak. The following is an excerpt from a speech I have given at the New York Stock Exchange on the occasions when our companies went public:

"We are standing in the halls of the institution that represents the economic system that lifted mankind out of poverty. My wife and I are thankful to be here and participate in the economic process that allows companies like ours to prosper by adding value to our customers, both the investors and the users of our capital whose real estate we finance. Capitalism, with all of its failings and all of its shortcomings has made this possible and is the economic anchor in America's democracy that has allowed her to become the most powerful country in the world. In the end I believe it is the system that has and will continue to raise the living standard of the world."

It is the combination of political and economic freedom that creates democratic capitalism, which makes up the economic and cultural environment of America. This system combines an incentive-driven market economy, a strong legal framework that values individual property rights, a representative government that respects the rights of individuals to life, liberty, and the pursuit of happiness, and a system of cultural institutions moved by the principles of liberty and justice for all. These converging ideas provide Americans with unlimited possibilities for economic success and the freedom to voluntarily contribute to our society, thus creating more opportunities for succeeding generations. It will be the fulfillment of one of my life's dreams if you, the Fleischer Scholars, never give up on your own dreams and press forward until they are accomplished.

EPILOGUE – A MISSION FOR THE FLEISCHER SCHOLARS

This book has attempted to tell the story of a life of continuous learning. It reflects how early awareness and application of basic principles can be life changing and enriching. My wife and I are forever grateful to have had the opportunity to live, work, and enjoy the lifestyle that America affords, which is made possible because of this country's underlying structure of personal liberty, democracy, the rule of law, and free capital markets. We are hopeful that the Mental Balance Sheet principles and experiences described in this book will be useful to the young Fleischer Scholars to whom we are dedicating it. It is our privilege to do so.

We believe that we will never achieve the "American dream" until we find ways, through knowledge, to bring socio-economically disadvantaged youngsters into the mainstream of American life. Among your generation are the future leaders of this great country. The Fleischer Scholars Program is our contribution toward that goal. We have found this effort to be one of the most fulfilling and rewarding of our lives. Therefore, it is our goal to touch, inform, and motivate as many qualified young lives as we can.

The fact that you were selected to participate in the Fleischer Scholars Program reflects that you are a very special person, of high intelligence and with your own unique talents. It is my hope that the program and this book have helped you to understand how to build the assets of your Mental Balance Sheet as you pursue your life's journey, and that you will go to college to learn how to learn, how to write, how to solve problems, and how to add assets to your Mental Balance Sheet.

You are uniquely qualified to know which of your friends could also benefit from the principles you have been taught in this program. It is my hope that you will reach out to other qualified students and get them involved. Find those who qualify, and together we'll all make the world a better place. It starts with us, and you can spread it. You may think to yourself, "I'm just one person! How can I make the world a better place?" I believe the following well-known story illustrates how you can do so:

There was once a wise man that used to go to the ocean to do his writing. He had a habit of walking on the beach before he began his work. One day, as he was walking along the shore, he looked down the beach and saw a human figure moving like a dancer. He smiled to himself at the thought of someone who would dance to the day, and so, he walked faster to catch up. As he got closer, he noticed that the figure was that of a young man, and that what he was doing was not dancing at all. The young man was reaching down to the shore, picking up small objects, and throwing them into the ocean.

He came closer still and called out "Good morning! May I ask what it is that you are doing?"

The young man paused, looked up, and replied, "Throwing starfish into the ocean."

"I must ask, then, why are you throwing starfish into the ocean?" asked the somewhat startled wise man.

To this, the young man replied, "The sun is up and the tide is going out. If I don't throw them in, they'll die."

Upon hearing this, the wise man commented, "But, young man, do you not realize that there are miles and miles of beach and there are starfish all along every mile? You can't possibly make a difference!"

At this, the young man bent down, picked up yet another starfish, and threw it into the ocean. As it met the water, he said, "It made a difference for that one."[1]

My challenge to you as a Fleischer Scholar is to improve the life of one of your friends. Share with your friend the knowledge, skills and values you have learned from this program, and together we can touch the lives of others and leave this world a better place than we found it.

To the world you may be just one person,
But to one person you may be the world.
---Author Unknown

In closing, I would like to point out a message that I read in college and have remembered for 60 years. It was in my philosophy class on Religions of the East and West. I believe that it was a Sanskrit writer who noted that pursuit of personal and material achievement, when morally balanced, was certainly acceptable for the majority of your life. However, in your twilight years you should attempt to make positive contributions that will exist beyond you, that will add value. I think of it as leaving this world a better place than you found it. And for me, that's what the Fleischer Scholars Program is about. You can begin the process right now—no need to wait until your twilight years—with one of your qualified friends.

I've held the idea planted by that Sanskrit writer in my mind for all these years. I'm not a priest or a rabbi. I'm a businessman and financier, a rancher, philanthropist, an art collector, and a renaissance man. I'm very simple in some ways, and probably more complex than I let on in others—as are you. All of the things that make us unique also make us the kind of people who can first put ourselves on a firm footing, then reach out to help others get themselves there. Let me and the Fleischer Scholars Program team help you, so you can help others.

Morton Fleischer

CHAPTER NOTES

[1] Eiseley, Loren. *The Unexpected Universe.* "The Star Thrower." Mariner Books. Reprint edition (October 18, 1972).

36465969R00128

Made in the USA
Middletown, DE
15 February 2019